English Grammar Practice

Contents

Introduction

New Round-Up 4 English Grammar Practice combines games and fun with serious, systematic grammar practice. It is ideal for young learners in the preliminary stages of English language learning.

Students see grammar points clearly presented in colourful boxes and tables. They practise grammar through lively, highly illustrated games and oral and writing activities.

New Round-Up is especially designed for different students studying English in different ways.

It can be used:
- in class with a coursebook. Students do both oral work — in pairs and in groups — and written work in New Round-Up.
- after class. The 'write-in' activities are ideal for homework. Students can practise what they have learned in the classroom.
- on holidays for revision. New Round-Up has clear instructions and simple grammar boxes, so students can study at home without a teacher.

The New Round-Up Teacher's Guide includes a full answer key, quizzes, tests plus answer keys, and audio scripts of progress check listening tasks.

2 **Listen and repeat. Then act out.**

Why are you standing in the rain, Sam? People don't usually stand in the rain. They can catch a cold.

I know that Mum but Dad says it's raining cats and dogs today and I want to catch a little puppy.

Present Simple is used:	**Present Continuous is used:**
• **for permanent situations.** She **works** in an office.	• **for temporary situations.** He**'s looking** for a new job these days.
• **for repeated or habitual actions in the present, especially with adverbs of frequency.** He often **buys** her flowers.	• **for actions happening at or around the time of speaking.** Chris **is painting** the garage at the moment.
• **for general truths and laws of nature.** The Sun **sets** in the west.	• **with *always* to express annoyance or criticism.** He's **always telling** lies!
• **for timetables or programmes.** The lesson **starts** at 10 o'clock.	• **for fixed arrangements in the near future.** I'm **flying** to London **tomorrow**. (It's all arranged. I've already bought the tickets. The time of the action is always stated or understood.)

Time Expressions with the present simple	**Time Expressions with the present continuous**
usually, always, never, often, sometimes, every day / week / month / year, on Mondays / Tuesdays, in the morning / afternoon / evening, at night / the weekend, etc.	now, at the moment, at present, this week / month, these days, today, tonight, tomorrow, next week, etc.

Adverbs of Frequency

Adverbs of frequency (often, always, usually, sometimes, rarely / seldom, never, etc.) **are placed before main verbs but after auxiliary / modal verbs** (be, have, can, will, must, shall, etc.)**.**
He **often goes** to the theatre.   He **is never** late.   Tonia **doesn't usually go** to bed late.

1 Present Simple – Present Continuous

1 Write the verbs in the third person singular.

1 I miss – he *misses*.....................
2 I buy – she ....
3 I carry – he ....
4 I fix – he ....
5 I watch – she ....

6 I call – he ....
7 I go – he ....
8 I dry – she ....
9 I play – he ....
10 I see – he ....

2 Put the verbs in the correct column in the third person singular, then say.

match	ring	teach	eat	cry	take
try	keep	rise	arrive	lose	like
bake	hit	care	begin	choose	sleep

/ s / after / f /, / k /, / p /, / t /	/ ɪz / after / s /, / ʃ /, / tʃ /, / dʒ /, / z /	/ z / after other sounds
bakes,	*matches,*	*tries,*

3 Look at the table, then ask and answer questions as in the example:

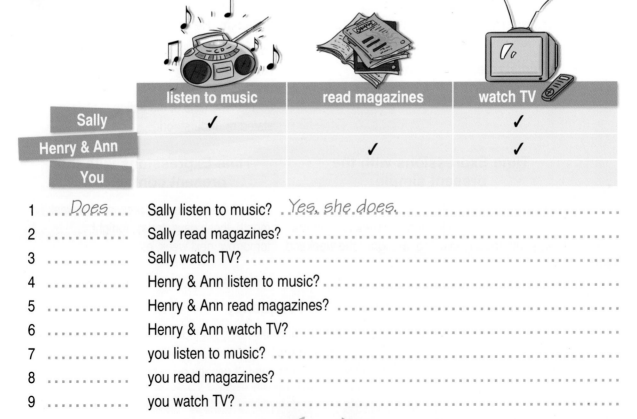

	listen to music	read magazines	watch TV
Sally	✓		✓
Henry & Ann		✓	✓
You			

1 ...*Does*... Sally listen to music? *Yes, she does.*.............
2 .... Sally read magazines? ....
3 .... Sally watch TV? ....
4 .... Henry & Ann listen to music? ....
5 .... Henry & Ann read magazines? ....
6 .... Henry & Ann watch TV? ....
7 .... you listen to music? ....
8 .... you read magazines? ....
9 .... you watch TV? ....

Present Simple – Present Continuous

4 **Match the verb forms in the sentences (1–6) to the correct use (a–f).**

1 She **works** in a bank.
2 They usually **eat** out on Saturdays.
3 Wool **comes** from sheep.
4 The Sun **rises** in the east.
5 The bus **arrives** at 5 o'clock.
6 The film **starts** in ten minutes.

a a general truth
b a timetable
c a permanent situation
d a programme
e a repeated or habitual action
f a law of nature

5 **a) Put the verbs in brackets into the *present simple*.**

Jason is 12 years old and he 1) .... *lives* .... (live) in York. He 2) .... (go) to school every day by bus. Jason's mother 3) .... (teach) German at university and his father 4) .... (work) in a bank.

In his free time, Jason 5) .... (play) football with his friends. He 6) .... (want) to be a football player when he grows up.

At weekends, Jason 7) .... (not/wake up) early. After lunch, he and his dad often 8) .... (play) board games or 9) .... (ride) their bicycles. Later in the day, his mum usually 10) .... (take) him to visit his best friend, Henry, and they 11) .... (spend) the evening watching films.

b) In pairs, ask and answer as in the example:

A: .How. old. is. Jason? ....
B: .He's. 12. years. old.. Where. does. he. live? ....
A: .He. lives. in. York,.. etc. ....

6 **Put the verbs in brackets into the *present simple*.**

1 A: What .... *does Peter do* .... (Peter/ do)?
   B: He .... (work) as a computer technician for LT & Company.
2 A: .... (your brother/ exercise)?
   B: Yes. He .... (go) jogging three times a week.

3 A: What time .... (the play/start)?
   B: At 6 o'clock. We need to hurry!
4 A: How long .... (koalas/live)?
   B: They .... (live) for about 15 years.
5 A: My dad .... (not/like) working out in the gym.
   B: Really? Mine .... (love) weightlifting and using the pool.

1 Present Simple – Present Continuous

7 Complete the sentences in order to make the statements true. Use *don't* / *doesn't* where necessary. Compare with your partner.

1 Rain .... *falls* .... (**fall**) from clouds.
2 Kangaroos . . . . (**live**) in Germany.
3 Yoghurt . . . . (**come**) from plants.
4 Water . . . . (**boil**) at 100°C.

5 Sheep . . . . (**eat**) grass.
6 Tomatoes . . . . (**grow**) on trees.
7 Cows . . . . (**lay**) eggs.
8 Plants . . . . (**need**) water to grow.

8 Put the adverbs of frequency in the correct place in the sentences.

1 Mark goes fishing with his grandfather.
(**rarely**) *.Mark rarely goes fishing.*
with his grandfather. . . . .
2 I don't play basketball at weekends.
(**always**) . . . .
. . . .
3 Does Fred help his mother with the
housework? (**often**) . . . .
. . . .
4 Ivan is at work on time. (**never**) . . . .

5 Does Layla read books in her free time?
(**usually**) . . . .
. . . .
6 I meet my friends at the shopping centre.
(**sometimes**) . . . .
. . . .
7 Sophie is at home on Sunday mornings.
(**always**) . . . .
. . . .
8 They go to the theatre. (**seldom**) . . . .
. . . .

9 Fill in *A* (always), *U* (usually), *O* (often), *S* (sometimes), *R* (rarely) or *N* (never) to say how often you do these things at weekends. Then interview your partner and fill in his/her information. Ask and answer as in the example:

	You	Your partner
get up early	N	
clean your room		
surf the Net		
go to the cinema		
meet your friends		

A: *How often do you get up early at weekends?* . . . . . .
B: *I never get up early at weekends. How about you?*

10 3 Add *-ing* to the following verbs and put them into the correct column. Listen and check. Listen and repeat.

| ~~play~~ | drive | lie | read | cycle | ride | write | take | sleep |
| swim | run | put | travel | die | drink | fly | cut | tie |

+ ing	-ie → y + ing	-e → ing	double consonant + ing
playing,			

11 Choose a verb from the list and complete the text.

| read | lie | eat | cry | run | sing | play | fish | ~~sit~~ |

Laura 1) *..is. sitting .* under a sunshade. Two boys 2) .... around a sandcastle while their father 3) .... a newspaper. Two girls 4) .... ice cream while their mother 5) .... along with the radio. Some boys 6) .... football near a man who 7) .... Jim 8) .... on a beach towel. On his right, a baby 9) ....

12 In pairs, ask and answer questions about the text above.

A: *Is. Laura. running? ....*
B: *No, she isn't. She's. sitting. under. a. sunshade, etc. .....*

13 **Put the words in the correct order to make sentences.**

1 doing / homework / Betty and Ann / are / their

Betty and Ann are doing their homework.

2 children / TV / are / watching / the?

....

3 not / going / I / am / tonight / out

....

4 biting / you / always / nails / are / your!

....

5 next week / house / are / they / moving

....

6 is / at / week / aunt's / staying / this / Beth / her / house

....

7 Lucy / tidying / not / room / now / her / is

....

8 they / what / are / doing?

....

14 **Look at the visual prompts. Complete the sentences using the verbs: *go*, *have*, *visit*, *play*.**

Mum,
I'm at Laura's house with Kelly.
Jane

You're Invited!!
Event: Deborah's Sweet 16
Date: Saturday July 19th
Time: 6:00 pm
Place: Applebee's

RUGBY SUNDAY 1:00 pm

John,
meet me at the park at 4:00 pm this afternoon.
Bob

1 He ...... *is playing* ...... rugby at 1:00 pm on Sunday.

2 Jane and Kelly .... Laura now.

3 Deborah .... a birthday party on Saturday.

4 Bob .... to the park this afternoon.

15 **Answer the questions in the negative as in the example. Use your own ideas.**

1 Are you doing your homework?
No. I'm not. I'm writing in my diary.

2 Is your mother at the supermarket right now?

....

3 Are you having a party on Saturday?

4 Is your dad working on his laptop now?

....

5 Are your parents going to the cinema tonight?

....

6 Is your sister talking on her mobile right now?

....

16 Cathy wants to get fit, so she has decided to make some changes. Look at the pictures and tell your partner.

1 at lunchtime / eat burgers / have a salad

Cathy usually eats burgers at lunchtime but today she is having a salad.

2 after lunch / read comics / ride her bike

3 in the afternoon / eat chocolate / eat yoghurt

4 in the evening / watch TV / exercise at home

17 Work in pairs. Ask each other about your holiday arrangements. Talk about:

- where / go
- how / go
- what time / (plane) leave
- when / arrive
- where / stay
- why / want to go
- take / camera

A: *Where are you going on holiday?*
B: *I'm going to Rome, etc.*

18 Choose a time expression from the list to complete each sentence. More than one answer is possible.

never	tonight	always	at the moment
every day	on Fridays	now	

1 She .... *never* .... eats meat. She's a vegetarian.

2 Mother is reading the paper ....

3 They are going to a party ....

4 She .... goes out on Saturdays.

5 He drives to work ....

6 She is watching TV right ....

7 Tim goes to the gym ....

Present Simple – Present Continuous

19 **Put the verbs in brackets into the *present simple* or the *present continuous*.**

1 A: *Do you want* **(you/want)** to come
   over tonight to play computer games?
   B: Sorry, I can't. I .... **(go)** to
   the cinema with some friends from school.

2 A: .... **(Ann/talk)**
   on the phone?
   B: No, she .... **(do)**
   her homework right now.

3 A: How often .... **(you/go)**
   swimming?
   B: Three times a week.

4 A: Bob and Sophie ....
   (study) hard these days.
   B: Yes, I know. They ....
   (want) to pass their exams.

5 A: I'm so happy Jim! My parents and I ...
   .... **(go)** on holiday next week.
   B: That's great! Where ....
   .... **(you/go)**?

6 A: How long ....
   (it/take) to travel to London by plane?
   B: About three hours.

20 **Put the verbs in brackets into the correct form
of the *present continuous* or the *present simple*.**

Hi Marvin,

   I 1) *'m writing* **(write)** this letter from Portugal. I
2) .... **(be)** on holiday here with
my family and we 3) .... **(have)** a
great time.
   Right now, I 4) .... **(lie)** on the beach. My little brother
5) .... **(play)** on the sand with his toys and my mother
6) .... **(watch)** him. My dad 7) .... **(swim)** in the sea.
I just love it here. We 8) .... **(get up)** late every day and
9) .... **(spend)** most of our time sunbathing.
   This afternoon we 10) .... **(go)** into town to do a little sightseeing.
Then my parents 11) .... **(take)** us to a nice restaurant. They
12) .... **(want)** us to try the local cuisine. I hope it tastes good!
   Well, that's all for now. See you when I get back!

Take care,
Wendy

21 **Complete the sentences so that they are true about you.**

1 I *have breakfast* in the morning.
2 My dad .... now.
3 My brother always ....

4 My parents .... at
   the moment.
5 My friend .... every day.

Stative Verbs

Some verbs rarely appear in the continuous tenses. These verbs express a permanent state and they are: appear (= seem), be, believe, belong, cost, feel, forget, hate, have (= possess), know, like, love, mean, need, prefer, realise, remember, see, seem, smell, sound, suppose, taste, think, understand, want, etc.

I **understand** it now.   **NOT**   I ~~am understanding~~ it now.

Some of these verbs can be used in continuous tenses but with a difference in meaning.

Present Simple	Present Continuous
I **think** he's Italian.	Tom **is thinking** of moving house.
(= believe)	(= is considering)
Katie **looks** happy.	They **are looking** at the paintings.
(= appears to be)	(= are taking a look at)
You can **see** the sea from my room.	Sam **is seeing** his friends tonight.
(= it is visible)	(= is meeting)
Derek **has** a new car.	We **are having** dinner at 8 o'clock.
(= possesses)	(= are eating)
This pie **tastes** really good.	Paul **is tasting** the soup to see if it needs salt.
(= it has a really good flavour)	(= is trying)
This new dress **fits** her perfectly.	He **is fitting** a new lock on the door.
(= it is her size)	(= is attaching)
He **is** so polite.	He **is being** so rude today!
(= that's his character)	(= he is behaving like that only today)
She **appears** to be tired.	She **is appearing** in a new TV show.
(= seems)	(= is taking part)

22 Put the verbs in brackets into the *present simple* or the *present continuous*.

1 A: I ..... *see* ...... (see) you still have a toothache.

   B: Yes, I do. Actually, I .... (see) my dentist later.

2 A: I .... (think) of visiting Jim this afternoon.

   B: Don't bother. I .... (think) he's on a business trip.

3 A: Why .... (Greg/be) so rude today?

   B: I have no idea. He .... (be) usually very polite.

4 A: Why .... (you/taste) the sauce? Does it need more pepper?

   B: No. It .... (taste) great the way it is.

5 A: Why .... (you/smell) the milk?

   B: Because it .... (smell) off. We should throw it away.

6 A: I see you .... (have) a new mobile phone.

   B: Yes, but I .... (have) trouble understanding how it works.

① **Present Simple – Present Continuous**

23 Use the verbs to complete the sentences. Use the *present simple* or the *present continuous*.

fit	look	have	smell	think
appear	~~prefer~~	not/know	not/like	not/belong

1 Aya ......*prefers*...... classical music to jazz and pop.

2 He .... new cabinets in the kitchen.

3 She .... so relieved now that the test is over.

4 Tom .... Indian food. It's too hot and spicy for him.

5 The new rock band .... on stage tonight.

6 This isn't Ahmed's coat. It .... to him.

7 The food .... nice.

8 The funfair rides are exciting. We .... a great time!

9 I .... where Jane is at the moment.

10 The Browns .... of going to the theatre tonight.

24 Underline the correct item.

1 The children **are having** / **have** so much fun at the circus!

2 Fiona **is looking** / **looks** at some photos.

3 This jacket **is fitting** / **fits** you perfectly. You should buy it.

4 Ron **is wanting** / **wants** to become a pilot.

5 I **am not understanding** / **don't understand** the meaning of that word.

6 He **is loving** / **loves** playing football.

7 I **am thinking** / **think** of buying a new CD.

What are you doing?

Imagine you are at home. In teams, students ask you questions to find out where you are and what you are doing.

• kitchen • bathroom • bedroom • living room

Team A S1: Are you in the living room?
Leader: Yes, I am.
Team A S2: Are you watching TV?
Leader: No, I'm not, etc.

Speaking Activity

(Talking about actions happening now)

Look at the picture. Ask and answer questions as in the examples:

- look / map
- take / pictures
- look at / postcards
- drink / coffee
- feed / birds
- eat / sandwich
- read / book

A: What's Mr Jones doing?
B: He's looking at a map.

A: Is Andy reading a book?
B: No, he isn't. He's taking pictures, etc.

Writing Activity

Imagine you are on holiday. Complete the email below telling your English pen friend about your holiday.

Greetings from . . . . ! We're staying at . . . .
The weather is . . . . There isn't a cloud in the sky.
Right now, I . . . . My parents . . . .
. . . . and my . . . .
We . . . . late every day and . . . .
. . . .
In the evening, we . . . . or . . . .
Tonight we . . . .
We love it here. There is so much to see and do. See you in . . . .
Yours,

. . . .

Past Simple – Present Perfect

When *did you start* writing novels?

Have you sold anything so far?

I *started* writing novels two years ago.

Yes – my colour TV, all the furniture, the carpets, my house...

Past Simple: verb + -ed

Past Simple is used:

- **for actions which happened at a stated time in the past.**
  He **sold** his car two weeks ago. (When? Two weeks ago.)

- **to express a past state or habit.**
  When he **was** young, he **lived** in a small flat.

- **for past actions which happened one after the other.**
  She **put on** her coat, **took** her bag and **left** the house.

- **for an action which happened in the past and cannot be repeated.**
  I once **spoke** to Princess Diana. (I won't see her again; she's dead.)

Present Perfect: have + past participle

Present Perfect is used:

- **for actions which happened at an unstated time in the past.**
  He **has sold** his car. (When? We don't know.)

- **to express actions which have finished so recently that there's evidence in the present.**
  He **has just painted** the room. (The paint is wet.)

- **to talk about experiences.**
  He **has tried** skydiving.

- **for actions which started in the past and continue up to the present.**
  She **has lived** in this house for two years. (She still lives in this house.)

  BUT He **lived** in Australia for one year. (He doesn't live in Australia now.)

- **for an action which happened in the past and may be repeated.**
  I've **met** Leona Lewis. (I may meet her again; she's still alive.)

Time adverbs and expressions used with the past simple	**Time adverbs and expressions used with the present perfect**
yesterday, last week / month / year / Monday, etc., ago, how long ago, just now, then, when, in 2000, etc.	just, ever, never, always, already, yet, for, since, so far, how long, lately, recently, today, this week / month / year, once, several times, etc.

Note:

Since is used to express a starting point.
I've known Ann **since** October.

For is used to express a period of time.
I've known Mary **for** two months.

Yet is used in questions and negations.
Have you met him **yet**? I haven't met him **yet**.

Already is used in statements and questions.
I've **already** posted the letters.

Just + present perfect
I've **just called** the doctor.

Just now + past simple
He **left just now**.

① Add -(e)d to the verbs and put them in the correct column.

~~cry~~	~~hate~~	fry	type	destroy	beg	play	enjoy
~~stay~~	taste	dance	plan	pray	try	study	empty
~~stop~~	prefer	like	annoy	phone	tip	travel	tidy

-e → + -d	double consonant + -ed	consonant + y → -ied	vowel + -y → -ed
hated,	*stopped,*	*cried,*	*stayed,*

② 🎧 5 Add -(e)d to the verbs and put them in the correct column. Listen and check. Listen and repeat.

~~add~~	wash	help	plan	love	laugh
~~open~~	rain	want	marry	end	hope
~~work~~	need	count	close	invite	kiss

/ ɪd / after / t /, / d /	/ t / after / k /, / s /, / tʃ /, / f /, / p /, / ʃ /	/ d / after other sounds
added,	*worked,*	*opened,*

3 **Put the verbs in brackets into the correct form of the past simple. Then choose the right answer.**

QUIZ

1	e	It ....was.... **(be)** a dinosaur.
2		He .... **(paint)** the *Mona Lisa*.
3		He .... **(write)** *Hamlet*.
4		They .... **(be)** from Scandinavia.
5		He .... **(invent)** the telephone.
6		They .... **(make)** their first flight at Kitty Hawk, North Carolina.
7		He .... **(become)** the first astronaut to travel to outer space.
8		It .... **(begin)** in 1939.
9		They .... **(discover)** polonium and radium.

a Alexander Graham Bell
b The Wright brothers
c Pierre and Marie Curie
d William Shakespeare
e Tyrannosaurus Rex
f Yuri Gagarin
g The Vikings
h Leonardo da Vinci
i World War II

4 **Put the verbs in brackets into the correct form of the past simple as in the example:**

1 A: What 1) ....*did you do*.... **(you/do)** last night?
  B: I 2) .... **(go)** to the cinema.
  A: What film 3) .... **(you/see)**?
  B: *The Pink Panther II*.

2 A: Why 1) .... **(not/Emily/come)** to Terry's party yesterday?
  B: She 2) .... **(have)** to study for an exam.

3 A: I 1) .... **(read)** the book you 2) .... **(give)** me about dinosaurs.
  B: 3) .... **(you/like)** it?
  A: Yes. It 4) .... **(be)** very interesting.

4 A: Where 1) .... **(you/spend)** your summer holidays?
  B: We 2) .... **(go)** to Jamaica.
  A: Really? What 3) .... **(it/be)** like?
  B: Great!

5 Use the *past simple* form of the verbs in the list to fill in the gaps in the following sentences. Which sentences refer to:

- **actions which happened at a specific time in the past** • **past habits**
- • **people who are no longer alive** • **actions which happened one after the other in the past**

be	play	~~catch~~	spend	walk	buy

1 Shelly ...*caught*... the bus to school yesterday. .*action which happened at a specific time in the past*....

2 Heath Ledger .... a talented actor. ....

3 They left the cinema and .... to the train station. ....

4 Mark and his band .... at the concert hall last Saturday. ....

5 My father .... every summer in the countryside when he was a boy. ......

6 Larry .... computer games yesterday afternoon. ....

6 James is in Monaco with his family. Write what he *has* or *hasn't done*.

- • ~~visit the Oceanographic Museum~~ ✓
- • see the Opera de Monte-Carlo ✗
- • visit the Prince's Palace ✗
- • take lots of photos ✓
- • buy souvenirs for his friends ✗
- • walk along the harbour ✓

1 ..*James has visited the Oceanographic Museum.*................

2 ....

3 ....

4 ....

5 ....

6 ....

7 In pairs, ask and answer about Anna and yourself as in the example:

	meet a famous person	cook a foreign meal	have a bad dream	visit a foreign country	be on a roller coaster
Anna	never	once	several times	recently	many times
You					

A: ..*Has Anna ever met a famous person?*................

B: ..*No, she has never met a famous person.*................

🎧 **6** **Listen and repeat. Then act out.**

> **have gone to / have been to / have been in**
>
> He**'s gone to** London. (He hasn't come back yet. He is still in London.)
> He**'s been to** Paris once. (He's visited Paris. He's back now.) (Present Perfect of the verb 'to go')
> I**'ve been in** Athens for a month. (I am in Athens.) (Present Perfect of the verb 'to be')

8 **Fill in the gaps with:** *has / have gone to*, *has / have been to* or *has / have been in*.

1 You can't see Tom before Wednesday. He . . . . *has gone to* . . . . Denmark for a few days on business.

2 My sister . . . . Bristol for two months now.

3 Wendy isn't here at the moment. She . . . . the supermarket to buy some milk and eggs.

4 The Miltons . . . . Sweden twice.

5 Greg and Terry . . . . the park to play football. They'll be back by 6 o'clock.

6 Jenny's brother . . . . hospital since Monday.

7 . . . . you ever . . . . the opera?

8 Jim . . . . the cinema. He left an hour ago.

9 **Fill in:** *since, for, already, just* or *yet*.

1 John has . . *just* . . finished his homework. His books are still on the table.

2 I haven't seen Sarah . . . . 2007.

3 They haven't bought the tickets for the concert . . . .

4 We've lived here . . . . ten years.

5 He's . . . . come back from jogging and he's a bit tired.

6 We've . . . . seen that film. Can we watch something else?

10 **Write sentences about yourself. Use the *present perfect*.**

1 not play tennis since ...
. *I haven't played tennis since* .....
. *last weekend.* ....

2 live here for ...
....

3 have my pet dog for ...
....

4 know my best friend since ...
....

5 not go to the cinema for ...
....

6 not invite friends over since ...
....

11 **Put the verbs in brackets into the *present perfect* or the *past simple*.**

Did
you know?

1 Victoria Falls ..... *has been* ..... **(be)** a popular
tourist attraction for many years.

2 In 1855, David Livingstone, a Scottish explorer,
.... **(name)** the falls after Queen Victoria.

3 The African government .... **(open)** two
national parks near the falls to protect wild animals.

4 The Victoria Falls Bridge is one of the most famous bridges in the
world. It .... **(take)** just 14 months to build and .... **(be)**
ready in April, 1905.

5 Over 50,000 people .... **(try)** bungee jumping off the Victoria Falls Bridge so far.

12 **Put the verbs in brackets into the *present perfect* or the *past simple*.**

1 A: ... *Have you ever been* ....
   (you/ever/go) to India?
   B: Yes, I ....
   (go) there last summer.

2 A: ....
   (you/speak) to Chloe?
   B: No, she ....
   (go) to the post office. She ....
   .... **(not/come)** back yet.

3 A: ....
   (you/ever/eat) Mexican food?
   B: Yes, I ....
   (try) it for the first time last week.

4 A: I .... **(go)** to the
   new cinema yesterday.
   B: It's nice, isn't it? I ....
   .... **(go)** there a few times.

5 A: I ....
   .... **(not/see)** Sam for a long time.
   B: Really? He ....
   (be) at the swimming pool this morning.

6 A: ....
   (you/do) your project, Chris?
   B: Yes, Mum. I ....
   .... **(finish)** it an hour ago.

13 Fill in the gaps with time adverbs or expressions from the list below:

ago	how long	for	how long ago	ever	already
so far	just	since (x2)	yet		just now

1 They got married a month ..... *ago* ..... .

2 He hasn't called us ....

3 I've had this car .... a year.

4 Tim isn't here. He's ....
   gone out.

5 She's typed three letters ....

6 Has Camila .... lied to you?

7 .... have you been in Rome?

8 I've studied Maths .... 2006.

9 I've .... been to that new
   restaurant. It's really nice.

10 .... did he move house?

11 The boss came ....

12 Peter has been here ....
    5 o'clock.

14 Put the verbs in brackets into the *present perfect* or the *past simple*.

A: Hi, Sarah. I 1) ... *haven't seen* ...
   (not/see) you for a long time. Where
   2) .... **(you/be)**?

B: I 3) .... **(go)** to China
   to teach English.

A: Wow! How 4) .... **(be)**
   it?

B: Very nice! I 5) .... **(stay)**
   in Beijing and 6) .... **(teach)** eight-year-old children.

A: How 7) .... **(you/find)** teaching them?

B: Great! The children 8) .... **(be)** clever and 9) ....
   (learn) very quickly. What 10) .... **(you/be)** up to?

A: Nothing as interesting as that! I 11) .... **(just/finish)** my exams.

B: That's good. Do you have any plans for the summer?

A: Yes, I 12) .... **(buy)** a ticket to Italy. I'm planning to stay with
   my cousin, Sabrina, for a month.

B: That's great! Sabrina is a lot of fun. I'm sure you'll have a great time. Don't forget to send
   me a postcard.

A: Okay! Take care. Speak to you when I get back.

15 **In pairs, act out dialogues as in the example:**

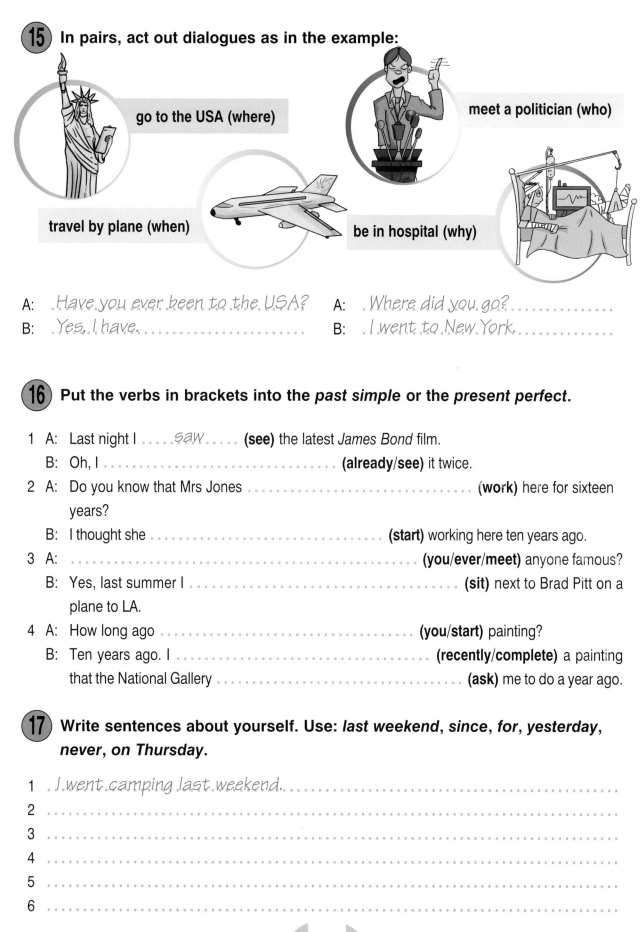

go to the USA (where)

meet a politician (who)

travel by plane (when)

be in hospital (why)

A: *Have you ever been to the USA?*   A: *Where did you go?*

B: *Yes, I have.*   B: *I went to New York.*

16 **Put the verbs in brackets into the *past simple* or the *present perfect*.**

1 A: Last night I ...... *saw* ...... **(see)** the latest *James Bond* film.

   B: Oh, I .... **(already/see)** it twice.

2 A: Do you know that Mrs Jones .... **(work)** here for sixteen
      years?

   B: I thought she .... **(start)** working here ten years ago.

3 A: .... **(you/ever/meet)** anyone famous?

   B: Yes, last summer I .... **(sit)** next to Brad Pitt on a
      plane to LA.

4 A: How long ago .... **(you/start)** painting?

   B: Ten years ago. I .... **(recently/complete)** a painting
      that the National Gallery .... **(ask)** me to do a year ago.

17 **Write sentences about yourself. Use: *last weekend*, *since*, *for*, *yesterday*,
never, *on Thursday*.**

1 *I went camping last weekend.*

2 ....

3 ....

4 ....

5 ....

6 ....

18 **Circle the mistake (A or B), then correct it.**

1 Frank <u>has done</u> his homework and then <u>listened</u> to music.   ...*did*...
   (A)   B
2 The children <u>have put</u> away their toys but they <u>didn't make</u> their beds yet.   ....
   A   B
3 Jim <u>learned</u> a lot since he <u>started</u> the language course.   ....
   A   B
4 Fatima <u>has finished</u> her lunch and then she <u>went</u> out to play.   ....
   A   B
5 They <u>haven't seen</u> each other since September when they <u>have met</u>
   A   B
   at Mary's party.   ....
6 Ryan <u>has bought</u> a new MP3 player yesterday but I <u>haven't seen</u> it yet.   ....
   A   B
7 The hockey player <u>hit</u> his head on Friday and he <u>was</u> in hospital since then.   ....
   A   B

19 **Put the verbs in brackets into the *past simple* or the *present perfect*.**

Dear Tina,

Hi! How are you? I'm having such a great time here in Singapore.
The city is so clean and the people are very kind and helpful!
We 1) ....*have been*.... **(be)** here for three days now and
we 2) .... **(do)** something different each
day. On Monday, we 3) .... **(go)** to the
shops in Singapore's Chinatown. I 4) ....
(buy) souvenirs for my friends and some CDs for me. On Tuesday, we
5) .... **(go)** on a riverboat tour on the
Singapore River. It 6) .... **(be)** fantastic!
Yesterday, we 7) .... **(visit)** Singapore Botanic Gardens. We
8) .... **(see)** many beautiful, exotic flowers and plants.

There are still a couple of things we 9) .... **(not/do)** yet. We
10) .... **(not/visit)** the Jurong Bird Park yet and we
11) .... **(not/go)** to the Singapore Zoo. We're going there
tomorrow. I can't wait to see the white Bengal tigers!

Singapore is a beautiful city! I 12) .... **(already/take)** so
many lovely photographs and I can't wait for you to see them when I get back.

See you next week.

Lots of love,
May

Speaking Activity

(Asking about experiences)

In pairs, ask and answer questions using the ideas below as in the example:

- ride a camel
- fly in a helicopter
- sleep in a tent
- go scuba diving
- win a competition

- see a famous person
- be on TV
- try sushi
- cook pasta

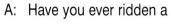

A: Have you ever ridden a camel?

B: No, I haven't. Have you?

A: Yes, I have.

B: Really? When was that?

A: Last summer, etc.

Writing Activity

Imagine you are in Disneyland. Complete the postcard below telling your English pen friend about your experiences. Use the phrases in the list.

- ride on roller coaster
- go on big wheel
- buy souvenirs

- visit haunted house
- meet Mickey Mouse / shake his hand

Dear . . . . ,

I'm great! I'm having lots of fun with my family here in Disneyland.
We've been here since Monday and so far we've done a lot of things.
We . . . .

Yesterday, I . . . .
It was very exciting!

There are still a couple of things we haven't done yet. We . . . .
. . . . and . . . .
But it's only Thursday and there is still plenty of time.

Well, that's all for now.

. . . .

Progress Check 1 (Units 1-2)

1 **Put the verbs in brackets into the *present simple* or the *present continuous*.**

Hi Isabel,

I'm in the beautiful city of Oxford. I 1) .*am studying*.. **(study)** German and Russian at the university here. I 2) .... **(find)** both languages interesting but German 3) .... **(be)** more difficult. All the other students on the course 4) .... **(feel)** the same way, too. We 5) .... **(meet)** once a week to discuss the lectures. This week, we 6) .... **(go)** to the theatre in London to see a play.

I 7) .... **(stay)** on the campus for the moment but a few of us 8) .... **(look)** for a house to share. The food in the halls 9) .... **(not/be)** very good, so we usually 10) .... **(have)** lunch at a restaurant nearby.

I hope to hear from you soon.

Take care,

Bill

2 **Put the verbs in brackets into the *past simple* or the *present perfect*.**

1 A: When ....*did you move*........
       (you/move) house, David?
   B: Three days ago but I ....
       .... **(not/unpack)** yet.
2 A: Do you like Chinese food?
   B: Actually, I ....
       (never/try) it.
3 A: I ....
       (just/finish) my essay.
   B: Really? I ....
       (write) mine yesterday evening.

4 A: How long ....
       (you/live) in America?
   B: I ....
       (come) here in 2004.
5 A: ....
       (you/type) the letters yet?
   B: Yes, I ....
       (finish) them half an hour ago and ....
       ....
       (give) them to Mr Harris.

3 **Fill in: *has / have been in / to, has / have gone to*.**

1 A: .*Have you ever been to*. France?
   B: No, I haven't but I'd like to go one day.
2 A: I'm afraid Sue and Pam can't come with
       us. They want to visit their grandmother.
   B: She ....
       hospital for a long time, hasn't she?

3 A: How long ....
       Mexico?
   B: For nearly three years.
4 A: Do you know where Mum is?
   B: I think she ....
       the post office to get some stamps.

24

4 Fill in: *yet*, *already*, *just*, *ago*, *yesterday*, *since*, *for*, *always*, *ever*, *how long* or *so far*.

1 Is it really a year ..... *since* ..... we last went on holiday?

2 I have .... finished my homework. I finished it two minutes ago.

3 Paul and Layla have visited three art galleries ....

4 Shakespeare was born over four hundred years ....

5 We have .... been to Canada so we are going to the USA this summer.

6 Jane has worked at this company .... six years.

7 .... have you known Petra and Charlie?

8 Olga woke up at 10 o'clock ....

9 He hasn't telephoned me ....

10 I have .... wanted to travel abroad.

11 Have you .... been to Disneyland?

5 Choose the correct item.

1 What are you cooking? It ...... very nice!
  A is smelling (B) smells C smelt

2 The stars ...... at night.
  A are shining B shines C shine

3 A: Do you play basketball at weekends?
  B: Yes, I ...... do.
  A never B often C seldom

4 ...... you go to the party yesterday?
  A Did B Do C Does

5 The next show ...... at 8:30 pm.
  A starting B starts C start

6 We left the concert hall three hours ....
  A before B last C ago

7 Have you ever ...... to Egypt?
  A be B been C gone

8 George ...... a bath at the moment.
  A is having B has C have

9 I ...... of buying a new car.
  A think B am thinking C thinks

10 The Sun ...... in the east.
  A is rising B rise C rises

11 Tina is happy because she ...... her exams.
  A passes B has passed C have passed

12 This apple pie ...... delicious!
  A taste B tastes C is tasting

13 A: Do you listen to the radio?
  B: Yes, I ...... do.
  A never B seldom C sometimes

14 Tommy usually ...... his homework after lunch.
  A do B does C doing

15 How long ...... you lived here?
  A are B were C have

16 Did you ...... Madame Tussauds while in London?
  A visiting B visits C visit

6 Put the words in the correct order to make sentences.

1 never / he / his wife's birthday / forgets
.He never forgets his wife's......
.birthday...........................

2 usually / she / wake up / early / doesn't
....
....

3 always / he / has / to travel abroad / wanted
....
....

4 rarely / he / at night / goes out
....

5 can't / always / you / want / get / what / you
....

6 beat / James / never / at tennis / can / I
....
....

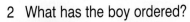

7 🎧 7 Listen and tick (✓) the correct box.

0 What is Tony doing now?

A ☐   B ☐   C ✓

3 What did Adam buy?

A ☐   B ☐   C ☐

1 What time does the bus arrive?

A ☐   B ☐   C ☐

4 What was the weather like?

A ☐   B ☐   C ☐

2 What has the boy ordered?

A ☐   B ☐   C ☐

5 What pets has Daniel got?

A ☐   B ☐   C ☐

Adjectives – Adverbs – Comparisons

8 **Listen and repeat. Then act out.**

Adjectives describe nouns. Adjectives have the same form in both singular and plural number. They normally come before nouns and after the verb 'to be'.
She's got three **lovely** children.
That car **is fast**. (What kind of car is it? A fast one.)

Adverbs describe verbs. They can describe how (adverbs of manner), where (adverbs of place), when (adverbs of time) or how often (adverbs of frequency) something happens.
He drives **carefully**. (How does he drive? Carefully.)

We usually form an adverb by adding -ly to an adjective.
slow-slow**ly**

Some adverbs are the same as their adjectives: hard, fast, early, daily, late, monthly.
He runs **fast**. He is a **fast** runner.

Some adverbs are irregular.
good - **well**   He's a good singer. He sings **well**.

---

1 **Write the correct adverb.**

→ -ly	-le → -ly	consonant + y → -ily
wide ......*widely*......	possible	busy ....
calm	simple	heavy ....
sad	terrible	happy ....

3 Adjectives – Adverbs – Comparisons

2 Put the words from the list below into the correct column.

~~bad~~	early	quick	tidy	hard	monthly
~~fast~~	easily	quietly	carelessly	late	careful
~~angrily~~	noisy	daily	slowly	large	happily

Adjectives	Adverbs	Adjectives & Adverbs
bad,	angrily,	fast,

3 🎧 9 Put the adverbs from the list below into the correct column.
Listen and check.

~~easily~~	here	often	happily
always	last year	there	carefully
yesterday	now	away	seldom
on Sunday	usually	everywhere	badly

How (adverbs of manner)	Where (adverbs of place)	When (adverbs of time)	How often (adverbs of frequency)
easily,			

Order of Adjectives

1 Opinion adjectives (bad, good, etc.) go before fact adjectives (old, red, etc.).
   She bought a **beautiful red** dress.
2 **When there are two or more fact adjectives, they go in the following order:**

	size	age	shape	colour	origin	material	noun
This is a	large	old	rectangular	brown	French	wooden	bed.

4 Put the adjectives in brackets in the correct order.

Hi Susan!

How was your birthday? Mine was great! We had a fancy dress party this year and I invited all

my close friends. I wore a 1) .....*funny orange*..... **(funny/orange)** clown suit

and 2) .... **(green/curly)** hair. Everyone laughed as I walked

around the room with my 3) .... **(red/plastic/huge)** shoes.

All my friends looked great too! My best friend Diane amazed us all with her fairy costume.

She wore 4) .... **(silver/shiny)** wings and carried a

5) .... **(long/plastic)** wand.

The party was a lot of fun. We listened to 6) ....

(new/cool) CDs and ate lovely desserts. Mum made 7) ....

(tasty/crunchy) toffee apples and 8) ....

(traditional/delicious) fairy cakes. We ended the night with a best costume contest and, to my
surprise, I won!

I will send you some photos very soon.

Take care,

Megan

5 Put the adjectives in the right order.

1 a new / woollen / red / smart / hat   *a smart, new, red, woollen hat* ....

2 a(n) modern / luxurious / Italian / car ....

3 two / long / blue / beautiful / dresses ....

4 a gold / tiny / round / Russian / coin ....

5 a plastic / blue / little / spoon ....

③ Adjectives – Adverbs – Comparisons

Order of Adverbs

- **Adverbs of frequency** (often, usually, etc.) go after auxiliary verbs but before main verbs. She **is never** late. He **never comes** late.
- **When there are more than two adverbs they go in the following order:**

	manner	place	time
She sat	lazily	by the pool	all day.

- **When there is a verb of movement, then the order is:**

	place	manner	time
He went	to Moscow	by plane	this morning.

---

6 **Underline the correct word, adjective or adverb.**

1 The children played **quiet** / <u>**quietly**</u>.

2 It was raining **heavy** / **heavily** yesterday.

3 She gave it a **careful** / **carefully** look.

4 She speaks **perfect** / **perfectly** German.

5 Have you seen Rebecca **recent** / **recently**?

6 He's a **slow** / **slowly** runner.

7 She sings **good** / **well**.

8 She bought a **nice** / **nicely** dress.

---

7 **Use the correct adjectives and adverbs to complete the exchanges.**

delicious	fancy	~~interesting~~

A: What did you do last night, Ben?

B: Nothing special. I just watched an 1) ...*interesting*... documentary on TV. What about you?

A: I met a friend from school and we went to a 2) .... restaurant. The food was really 3) ....

hard	last	well

A: How did you do in the race yesterday?

B: Not very 4) .... Although I tried 5) ...., I came in 6) ....

A: Cheer up. What matters is that you did your best.

confusing	really	hard

A: Did you finish your Maths homework, Camila?

B: Yes, Dad but it was 7) .... difficult. I had a 8) .... time understanding all the formulas.

A: I know. Some of them can be 9) .... Anyway, next time you have problems, just ask.

8 **Rewrite the sentences in the correct order.**

1 he / went / in the morning / to school / by bicycle *He went to school by bicycle in the morning.*

2 at breakfast / I / drink milk / always ....

3 goes to work / by bus / never / Diego ....

4 at school / yesterday / hard / I worked ....

5 his books / often / forgets / Tom ....

6 home / last night / they went / on foot ....

7 for an hour / in the queue / patiently / he waited ....

8 he goes / often / abroad / on business ....

10 **Listen and repeat. Then act out.**

What is redder than a tomato, louder than a roaring lion and blows off more steam than a kettle?

I haven't the slightest idea.

Easy, my mum.

Frank! Clean up your room!!!

Comparisons

Adjectives of:	Positive	Comparative	Superlative
one syllable	tall	tall**er** (than)	the tall**est** (of/in)
two syllables ending in -er, -ly, -y, -w	happy friendly	happ**ier** (than) friendl**ier** (than)	the happ**iest** (of/in) the friendl**iest** (of/in)
two or more syllables	modern beautiful	**more** modern (than) **more** beautiful (than)	the **most** modern (of/in) the **most** beautiful (of/in)

Spelling

Adjectives ending in:		
-e → -r / -st	-y → -ier / -iest	**one stressed vowel between two consonants – double the consonant**
larg**e** – larg**er** – larg**est**	heav**y** – heav**ier** – heav**iest**	big – bi**gg**er – bi**gg**est

③ Adjectives – Adverbs – Comparisons

⑨ Complete the table.

Adjectives	Comparative	Superlative
small	*smaller*	*the smallest*
....	better	....
loud	....	....
....	higher	....
intelligent	....	....
big	....	....
....	more helpful	....
....	....	the fastest

Now complete the sentences with adjectives from the table.

1 I can't reach the vase. Why did Dad put it on .... *the highest* .... shelf?
2 This is .... essay I've ever written.
3 Steve's voice is .... than Tim's.
4 Judy is .... than Ben. After all she's a straight-A student.
5 Asia is .... than Africa.
6 The cheetah is .... animal in the world.

Comparisons of Adverbs

	Positive	Comparative	Superlative
adverbs with the same form as adjectives	fast	fast**er**	the fast**est**
two syllable adverbs ending in -y	early	earl**ier**	the earl**iest**
two-syllable or compound adverbs	often clearly	**more** often **more** clearly	the **most** often the **most** clearly

Irregular Comparatives and Superlatives

Positive	Comparative	Superlative
good / well	better	best
bad / badly	worse	worst
much	more	most
many / a lot of	more	most
little	less	least
far	further / farther	furthest / farthest

a) **further / farther (adv) = longer (in distance)**
His house is **further / farther** away from the bus stop than mine.
further (adj) = more
For **further** information, see the secretary.

b) **very + positive degree**
   much + comparative degree
It's **very cold** today.
It's **much colder** today than yesterday.

10 Use the adverbs in the list in the correct form to complete the sentences. Add any necessary words.

fast	formally	early
well	~~wonderfully~~	carefully

1 This is .... *the most wonderfully* .... written book I've ever read.
2 David cooks .... his wife.
3 Sam drives .... all my friends. He always pays attention to the road signs.
4 Susan is .... dressed .... Joanna.
5 Chloe arrived .... the other students.
6 Klaus ran .... and won the race.

11 Write *comparatives* or *superlatives* and then answer the questions. Check your answers.

Quiz

1 Which is ..... *the hottest* ... **(hot)** planet in the solar system?
   a) Venus   b) Jupiter

2 Is the Sahara Desert ....
   (small) than the Kalahari Desert?
   a) yes   b) no

3 Can an eagle see ....
   (good) than a human?
   a) yes   b) no

4 Which is .... **(long)** wall in the world?
   a) the Wall of Dubrovnik
   b) the Great Wall of China

5 Is Mount Everest ....
   (high) than Mount Kilimanjaro?
   a) yes   b) no

6 Which is .... **(tall)** building in the world?
   a) Taipei 101 Tower   b) Burj Dubai Tower

7 Does the blue whale make a ....
   (loud) sound than the dolphin?
   a) yes   b) no

8 Which animal runs ....
   (fast) than the leopard?
   a) the cheetah
   b) the lion

2b 3a 4b 5a 6b 7a 8a

3 Adjectives – Adverbs – Comparisons

12 Put the adjectives in brackets into the *comparative* or *superlative* form.

Dear Robert,

I'm writing to tell you about our new house. It's lovely! It's 1) ..... *the nicest* ..... **(nice)** house I have ever seen. It's much 2) .... **(big)** than our last one but also 3) .... **(expensive)**. The house looks very modern. There are many rooms with large windows and wooden floors.

I finally have a room that I don't have to share with my 4) .... **(young)** brother. My bedroom is on the second floor and I have a great view. 5) .... **(good)** thing about this house is that it has a lovely garden. There are lots of flowers and trees around which make the place much 6) .... **(colourful)**.

The new house is in a peaceful area. It's actually 7) .... **(quiet)** area I've ever lived in. The neighbours are also very kind. Can you believe they organised a party for us? They are definitely 8) .... **(friendly)** people I have ever met.

Well, that's all my news. I hope you'll visit me soon. I can't wait to show you the new place.

Yours,

Chris

13 Use *What's* or *Who's* and the adjectives in brackets in the *superlative* to complete the questions. Then ask and answer in pairs.

1 .*What's the most exciting*...... **(exciting)** sport to play?
.*I think it's football.*....................................

2 .... **(funny)** comedian in the world?
....

3 .... **(good)** programme on TV?
....

4 .... **(popular)** singer in your country?
....

5 .... **(difficult)** language in the world?
....

Types of Comparisons

£600
£200

£1100
£2700
£1200

The armchair is **as comfortable as** the sofa but it **isn't as expensive as** the sofa.

The ring is **less expensive than** the necklace. The earrings are **the least expensive of** all.

The more he studies, **the better** student he becomes.

1	**as** ...(positive)... **as** **not so / as** ...(positive)... **as**	Paul is **as heavy as** Tom. Jane is **not so / as tall as** Mary.
2	**less** ...(positive)... **than** **the least** ...(positive)... **of / in**	Betty is **less hard-working than** Kate but Jean is **the least hard-working of** all.
3	**the** + comparative ..., **the** + comparative	**The harder** you work, **the more** money you earn.

14 Use the adjectives to write comparisons as in the example:

heavy	dangerous	fierce	fast

1 An elephant *is heavier than a tiger.*
  An elephant *is less dangerous than a tiger.*
  A tiger is *fiercer than an elephant.*
  An elephant isn't *as fast as a tiger.*

expensive	cheap	slow	comfortable

2 A car is ....
  A bicycle is ....
  A car isn't ....
  A bicycle is ....

friendly	quiet	intelligent	playful

3 A dog is ....
  A cat is ....
  A dog is ....
  A cat isn't ....

3 Adjectives – Adverbs – Comparisons

15 **Put the adjectives / adverbs in brackets into the *comparative* or *superlative* form, adding any necessary words.**

1 A: I like Geometry more than Algebra. What about you?

B: Actually, I find Algebra much ...*more interesting*... **(interesting)**.

2 A: What did you think of the Chemistry exam, Peter?

B: Well, it was .... **(difficult)** exam we've had so far.

3 A: Were the tickets for the concert expensive?

B: No, I got seats in the back row. They were .... **(cheap)** I could find.

4 A: Your work isn't very good, Elisha. I'm sure you can do .... **(well)**.

B: I promise I'll try .... **(hard)**.

5 A: Thank you for your help.

B: My pleasure. For .... **(far)** information, contact the school.

6 A: Do you prefer the brown jacket?

B: Yes, but it is much .... **(expensive)** the grey one.

7 A: We can't hear you. Could you speak .... **(loudly)**, please?

B: Yes, of course.

16 **Complete the sentences using the words in brackets in the correct form. Which of the sentences 1–6 don't you agree with? Correct them.**

1 Comics are ...*more interesting*....
...*than*........ **(interesting)** fairy tales.

2 Burgers are as ....
.... **(tasty)** tacos.

3 Skating is ....
.... **(difficult)** cycling.

4 Rock climbing is as ....
.... **(dangerous)** surfing.

5 Football is .... **(popular)**
.... basketball.

6 Sailing is ....
.... **(relaxing)** golf.

17 **Complete the sentences using *the + comparative* as in the example:**

1 The wind blew hard. The kite flew high in the sky.
......*The harder*...... the wind blew, ...*the higher*...... the kite flew.

2 It got dark. I became frightened.
.... it got, ... I became.

3 We worked hard. We became very successful.
.... we worked, ... we became.

4 The boys got noisy. Their father became angry.
.... the boys got, ... their father became.

Too – Enough

Too comes before adjectives. It has a negative meaning and shows that something is more than enough, more than necessary or more than wanted.

- **too + adjective + to-infinitive**
  The tea is **too hot to drink**. (It's so hot that we can't drink it.)

The baby is **too young** to walk. (He can't walk.)

Enough comes before nouns but after adjectives. It has a positive meaning and shows that there is as much of something as wanted or needed.

- **adjective + enough**
  enough + noun } **+ to-infinitive**
  Her house is **big enough** to have a party.
  (She can have a party at her house.)
  They have **enough money to go** on holiday this summer.
  (They can go on holiday.)

- **not ... enough + to-infinitive (negative meaning)**
  She is **not strong enough to carry** her bike.
  (She can't carry her bike.)

Mandy is **old enough to drive** a car. (She can drive a car.)

- **too ... (for somebody/something) + to-infinitive (negative meaning)**
  This ring is **too expensive for me to buy**. (The ring is very expensive, I can't buy it.)

Too much – Too many – Not enough

There's **too much traffic** today. **(Uncountable)**
There are **too many cars** in the streets. **(Countable)**

There **isn't enough butter** left. **(Uncountable)**
There **aren't enough chairs**. **(Countable)**

---

18 **Complete the sentences with *too* or *enough*.**

1 You can't borrow my car. You aren't old
  ...*enough*... to drive.

2 I'm sorry Tim but I can't meet you this week.
  I'm .... busy.

3 Can you help me with these boxes? I'm not
  strong .... to lift them.

4 I haven't got .... money. Can
  you lend me some?

5 I'm .... tired to go to the gym
  this evening.

6 Let me help you. You aren't tall ....
  .... to reach the top shelf.

7 This video game is ....
  expensive for me to buy.

8 There aren't .... parks in the
  city for children to play.

19 **Complete the responses using *too* or *enough*.**

1 A: Can you walk to the restaurant? **(close)**
   B: *Yes, it is close enough.*

2 A: Can Wendy do these exercises? **(difficult)**
   B: *No, they're too difficult.*

3 A: Can we buy this sofa? **(cheap)**
   B: Yes, ...

4 A: Can baby Annie walk yet? **(young)**
   B: No, ...

5 A: Can she carry this suitcase? **(light)**
   B: Yes, ...

6 A: Can Mario come out to play? **(busy)**
   B: No, ...

20 **Circle the correct word.**

1 Don't spend too (much)/ **many** time watching TV. You haven't finished your essay yet.

2 I haven't got **enough** / **much** eggs to make a cake.

3 You've spent too **many** / **much** money on these clothes.

4 There are too **many** / **much** flowers in the vase.

5 Jenny doesn't have **many** / **enough** money to buy a computer.

6 There isn't **much** / **many** jam left in the jar.

21 **Complete the exchanges with *too much* or *too many*.**

1 A: Can you see Sarah?
   B: No, there are ... *too many* ... people in front of me.

2 A: Please don't make .... noise. I'm trying to study.
   B: Okay, we promise to keep it down.

3 A: Did you pass your Science quiz?
   B: I don't think so. I made .... silly mistakes.

4 A: Are you coming out later?
   B: No, sorry. I have .... homework to do.

GAME

Compare

Play in teams. Use the adjectives and nouns to make sentences using the *comparative* form.

cars / bicycles, football / tennis, burgers / vegetables, cats / dogs

fast, friendly, entertaining, healthy, loyal, noisy, boring, tasty, dangerous, expensive, comfortable, popular

Team A S1: Cars are faster than bicycles.
Team B S1: Cats are less friendly than dogs, etc.

Speaking Activity

(Making comparisons)

Use the adjectives in the list to compare the means of transport in the pictures.

- comfortable • fast • cheap • dangerous • expensive • slow
- safe • relaxing

A: Which is more comfortable, a plane or a bus?
B: A plane is more comfortable than a bus.
A: And which is the most comfortable?
B: A train is the most comfortable of all, etc.

Writing Activity

How do you like to travel: by train or by bus? Write a short paragraph. Use the adjectives from the Speaking Activity.

I like travelling by .... because
.... and it
is much ....
.... isn't as
.... as
....
.... is too
....

'Will' – 'Be going to' – Future Continuous

 Listen and repeat. Then act out.

There's going to be a terrible snowstorm. You'll have to stay the night.

In that case I'll phone my parents.

Good idea. They will probably be worried if you don't phone them.

Oh no! It's not that! I'm going to ask them to bring me my nightclothes.

We use will and be going to to talk about the future.

Will is used:

- **to talk about things we are not sure about or we haven't decided yet.**
  I'll probably **buy** a new bike. (I'm not sure yet.)

- **to express hopes, fears, threats, on-the-spot decisions, offers, promises, warnings, predictions, comments, etc. especially with: expect, hope, believe, I'm afraid, I'm sure, I know, I think, probably, etc.**
  I'm hungry. I'll **make** a sandwich. (on-the-spot decision)

- **to make a prediction based on what we think or imagine.**
  I think you **will pass** the test.
  She **will** probably **phone** later.

- **to talk about actions which will definitely happen in the future and which we cannot control.**
  He **will be** twelve next year.

Be going to is used:

- **to talk about things we are sure about or we have already decided to do in the near future.**
  I'm going to buy a new bike.
  (I've decided it.)

- **to express intentions and plans.**
  Now that I've got the money, I'm going to buy a new dress. (intention)
  I'm going to get some more training so I can get a better job. (plan)

- **when we can see (evidence) that something is going to happen.**
  Watch out! We're **going to have** an accident.
  (We can see a car coming.)
  It's **going to rain**. (We can see dark clouds in the sky.)

Time expressions used with will – be going to

tomorrow, tonight, next week / month / year, in two days, the day after tomorrow, soon, in a week / month, etc.

'Will' – 'Be going to' – Future Continuous

1 **Read the sentences below and mark them as *a*, *b*, *c*, *d* or *e* according to what they express.**

1 I'm hungry. I'll make myself a sandwich. ...c...
2 Don't worry. I won't tell anybody. ....
3 Stop talking or I'll send you out. ....
4 Annie will be three years old next month. ....
5 I think it will rain today. ....
6 This dress is beautiful. I'll buy it. ....
7 We'll probably be home before dinner. ....
8 I promise I'll be on time. ....

a prediction based on what we think or imagine
b promise
c on-the-spot decision
d threat
e action which will happen in the future and we cannot control

2 **Complete the sentences.**

won't let   'll take   'll close   'll be   won't pass   'll catch

1 It's cold. I 'll close the window.
2 His teacher thinks he .... a great pianist one day.
3 Do your homework or I .... you go out.
4 I'm afraid she .... her exams.
5 Put on your coat or you .... a cold.
6 This shirt is nice. I .... it.

3 **Answer the questions about yourself using *I hope*, *I think*, *I believe*, *I expect*, *perhaps* or *probably* as in the example:**

1 Where will you go at the weekend?
   I'll probably go skiing in the mountains.
2 What will you buy your best friend for his/her birthday?
   ....
3 Where will you be at 3 o'clock tomorrow afternoon?
   ....
4 Who will you ask if you need help studying for exams?
   ....
5 Where will you spend your holidays?
   ....

4   'Will' – 'Be going to' – Future Continuous

Will	Shall
Will is used to express predictions, warnings, offers, promises, threats, requests, suggestions, on-the-spot decisions, opinions, hopes and fears (especially with words such as: think, expect, suppose, hope, believe, know and probably).	**Shall** is used with **I** or **We** in questions, suggestions and offers.
I expect she **will** come early. (prediction)	Shall we go by train? (suggestion) Shall I help you with your bags? (offer)

4   Fill in: *will*, *won't* or *shall*.

Larry: 1) ..... *Shall* ..... we go for a picnic tomorrow?

Sue: Yes. That's a good idea. I 2) .... make some sandwiches.

Larry: OK. And I 3) .... bring some lemonade.

Sue: 4) .... I buy some cheese?

Larry: I don't really like cheese.

Sue: I 5) .... buy any then. I 6) .... bring some fruit instead.

Larry: I think it 7) .... be sunny tomorrow so I 8) .... probably wear my shorts. I 9) .... take a pullover.

Sue: Well, I think I 10) .... take mine. It is still cold in the mornings.

5   What is going to happen? Use the phrases to complete the sentences.

- play tennis
- ~~watch a film~~
- make a cake
- wash the dishes
- win the race
- take the bus

1 They .are going to. .watch a film.

2 She ....

3 They.................

4 Bob ....

5 They.................

6 Emma ....

6 **Mrs Potter is the new music teacher at Braxton Academy. Look at the ideas and say what she is going to do as in the example:**

- offer new courses like *Electronic Music* and *Songwriting*
  She's going to offer new courses like Electronic Music and Songwriting.

- invite musicians to play for her students
  ....

- take the students to see the *London Symphony Orchestra*
  ....

- organise a concert at the end of the school year
  ....

7 **Use the words to make questions and then answer them.**

1 are / going / to / what / you / next / do / Sunday?
  What are you going to do next Sunday?
  I'm going to visit my grandparents.

2 going / buy / you / to / for / what / your / birthday / best friend's / are?
  ....

  ....

3 learn / are / a / going / language / new / you / to / year / next?
  ....

  ....

4 are / abroad / you / this / travel / summer / to / going?
  ....

  ....

Note:

- **We use the Present Continuous rather than 'be going to' for things which are definitely arranged to happen in the future.**
  They**'re having** a party next week. (It's all arranged. The invitations have already been sent.)
  They**'re going to have** a party in two weeks. (They've decided but it hasn't been arranged yet.)

- **We use the Present Simple for timetables, programmes, etc.**
  Our plane **leaves** at 10:30 am.

- **We do not use the Future tense after the words while, before, until, as soon as, if (conditional) and when (time conjunction). However, we can use when + will, if when is a question word.** Call me **when** you arrive.   **BUT**   **When will you be** ready?

- **With the verbs go and come we often use the Present Continuous rather than 'be going to'.** I'm going out tonight.   **RATHER THAN**   I'm going to go out tonight.

4 **'Will' – 'Be going to' – Future Continuous**

8 Fill in the *present continuous* or *be going to*, then identify the speech situations.

fixed arrangement – something already decided

1 *fixed arrangement.*

She *is getting married*
(get/married) this afternoon.

2 ....

They ....
.... **(get/married)** in June.

3 ....

He ....
(fly) to New York in an hour.

4 ....

He ....
(travel) to New York.

5 ....

She ....
(phone) the dentist.

6 ....

She ....
(see) the dentist tomorrow.

9 Put the verbs in brackets into the *present simple* or the *future simple*.

1 We ... *will leave* ... **(leave)** as soon as the taxi ... *arrives* ... **(arrive)**.

2 He .... **(phone)** us before he .... **(leave)** home.

3 She .... **(stay)** at home until she .... **(feel)** better.

4 "When .... **(you/visit)** them?" "Probably next week."

5 When Corey .... **(finish)** school, he .... **(go)** to university.

6 I .... **(send)** you a postcard as soon as I ....
(get) to Brazil.

7 When .... **(she/be)** back?

8 If you .... **(see)** Betty, tell her about the party.

10 Fill in: *shall*, *will* or *be going to*.

1 A: What do you want for lunch?
  B: I think I .... *will* .... have chicken and some salad.

2 A: Josh has come back from England.
  B: I know. I .... see him later today.

3 A: Costas and I .... get married in April.
  B: Really? Congratulations!

4 A: .... we meet on Sunday?
  B: Sorry, but I .... visit my aunt. She is expecting me.

5 A: Is Dave coming to the party?
  B: Yes, but he .... probably be late.

6 A: Have you decided where to go on holiday?
  B: Yes, I .... travel around Europe.

11 Look at the pictures and fill in the gaps with the verbs from the list in the *present continuous*, the *future simple (will)*, the *present simple* or *be going to*.

- eat   - buy   - have   - start   - see   - ~~be~~

1 "I hope I ...*'ll be*... on time for the meeting."

2 The film .... in twenty minutes.

3 "It's lovely. I .... it."

4 Annie .... some cake.

5 They .... a party for their 50th anniversary next Sunday.

6 "OK, Mum. I .... you at home, then."

'Will' – 'Be going to' – Future Continuous

12 Put the verbs in brackets into the *present simple*, the *present continuous*, *be going to* or *will*.

Gary: What 1) .are you planning. **(plan)** to do after the
exams? 2) .... **(you/stay)** in London?

Angela: No, I 3) .... **(leave)** this
weekend. I 4) .... **(visit)** my
brother in Wales. What about you?

Gary: I 5) .... **(think)** of getting a
part-time job. I 6) .... **(want)** to
buy a new electric guitar.

Angela: Oh, so 7) .... **(you/be)** still with your band?

Gary: Yes. In fact, we 8) .... **(play)** at Sam's Place this Friday. Can
you come?

Angela: Of course. My plane 9) .... **(not/leave)** until 8 pm on
Saturday so I 10) .... **(have)** plenty of time to pack.

Gary: Great!

Angela: Is it OK if I 11) .... **(bring)** a friend?

Gary: Of course. Invite as many people as you like.

Angela: Thanks. I 12) .... **(see)** you there.

13 Put the verbs in brackets into the *present simple*, the *present continuous*, *be going to* or *will*.

1 A: I .am seeing. **(see)** Jim at 8 o'clock
   tonight.
   B: Really? I thought he was away on a
   business trip.

2 A: Would you like something to drink?
   B: I .... **(have)**
   a glass of orange juice, please.

3 A: What time ....
   (the bus/leave)?
   B: In half an hour.

4 A: I don't understand this exercise, Dad.
   B: OK, Peter I ....
   (help) you.

5 A: Have you decided what to get Jim for his
   birthday?
   B: Yes. I .... **(buy)** him a watch.

6 A: I .... **(go)** to the cinema. There's
   a new film on. Would you like to come?
   B: What time ....
   (the film/start)?

7 A: Look at that car!
   B: Oh no! It ....
   (hit) the lamppost!

8 A: The Ting Tings ....
   (play) a concert at Wembley Stadium.
   B: I know. I have already bought a ticket.

Future Continuous

Affirmative	Negative	Interrogative
I will be working	I will not (won't) be working	Will I be working?
You will be working	You will not (won't) be working	Will you be working?
He will be working	He will not (won't) be working	Will he be working?
She will be working	She will not (won't) be working	Will she be working?
It will be working	It will not (won't) be working	Will it be working?
We will be working	We will not (won't) be working	Will we be working?
You will be working	You will not (won't) be working	Will you be working?
They will be working	They will not (won't) be working	Will they be working?

The Future Continuous is used:

- for an action which will be in progress at a stated future time.

> At 12 o'clock next Saturday, I'll be fishing with my grandson.

- for an action which will definitely happen in the future as the result of a routine or arrangement.

> I can give your message to Sue. I'll be seeing her later on today.

- when we ask politely about someone's plans for the near future. (What we want to know is if our wishes fit in with their plans.)

> Will you be driving to the party tonight?

> Yes. Why?

> Could you give me a lift, please?

14 Look at the pictures and use the ideas to make sentences as in the example:

1   I / play / hockey / 11 o'clock / next Tuesday
.. *I will be playing hockey at* ....
.. *11 o'clock next Tuesday.* ....

2   Next Monday, / we / fly / Disney World
....
....

3   This time next Sunday, / I / ski / with my friends
....
....

4   In a few weeks, / we / sail / in the Mediterranean
....
....

15 Put the verbs in brackets into the *future simple* or the *future continuous*.

Matt: How about going camping this weekend?

Jeff: Sounds great! I 1) *'ll call* **(call)** you this evening and we can talk more about it.

Matt: OK. Do you mind if I invite Henry?

Jeff: Of course not. Actually, I have a class with him later on so I 2) .... **(ask)** him.

Matt: Great! I 3) .... **(be)** home after 7:00 pm so I 4) ....
(talk) to you then.

Jeff: Perfect! Just think, in two days' time, we 5) ....
(sit) by a campfire roasting marshmallows.

Matt: And we 6) .... **(tell)** scary stories, too! I can
hardly wait!

16 Put the verbs in brackets into the *future simple*, *be going to* or the *future continuous*.

1 A: I'm too tired to do the washing-up.
  B: Don't worry! I *'ll do.* **(do)** it for you.

2 A: Will you come to the party on Saturday?
  B: No, I can't. I .... **(visit)** my grandparents.

3 A: Is Jason home?
  B: No. I think he .... **(be)** back late tonight.

4 A: Are you excited about your trip?
  B: Absolutely! This time tomorrow, I .... **(fly)** to Jamaica.

5 A: Why is Mark dressed in a suit?
  B: Because he .... **(meet)** Mr Rogers.

6 A: Did you tell Sophia about the party?
  B: Not yet. I ....
  (see) her at the meeting later on, so I
  .... **(tell)** her then.

7 A: How old is your son?
  B: He .... **(be)** six next month.

8 A: .... **(you/use)** the car tomorrow? I want to go shopping.
  B: I don't know yet.

9 A: Watch out! You .... **(fall)**!
  B: Don't worry. The ladder is safe.

10 A: What can I get you, madam?
   B: I .... **(have)** half a kilo of meat, please.

11 A: What are your plans for the summer?
   B: We .... **(go sailing)** in the Mediterranean.

12 A: .... **(you/go)** to the library later, Nadia?
   B: Yes. Do you want me to return your books?

17 Put the verbs in brackets into the *future simple*, *be going to* or the *future continuous*.

Dear Kimberly,

  I have great news! My family and I 1) *..are going to..* *...spend...* **(spend)** our summer holidays in Greece! We 2) .... **(travel)** there by boat.
  We 3) .... **(stay)** at my aunt's house. It's near the beach. This time next month, I 4) .... **(drink)** a glass of cold lemonade under the hot sun. Doesn't that sound great?
  I think my friend Sarah 5) .... **(come)** too but she isn't sure yet. Anyway, I have lots of cousins there, so I'm sure I 6) .... **(have)** a great time.
  I promise I 7) .... **(send)** you a lovely postcard when I get there.

Love,
Elena

Are you going to ...?

In teams, try to guess what the leader is going to do.
Each team can ask two questions.

Leader: I'm going to the kitchen.
Team A S1:   Are you going to make a sandwich? etc.

Speaking Activity

(Talking about future plans)

In pairs, discuss your plans for your summer holiday. Talk about:

- where / go
- where / stay
- how long / stay
- who / go with
- how / get there
- what / do

A: Are you doing anything on your summer holiday?
B: Yes, I'm going to a summer camp.
A: Great. Is anyone going with you?
B: I think my sister will come but she isn't sure yet, etc.

Writing Activity

Write a letter to your English pen friend about a trip you are planning to take.

Dear .... ,

How are you? I'm so excited! I'm writing to tell you about my summer holiday plans.
I .... by .... ! I ....
.... for .... This time next month, I
.... and ....
Doesn't that sound wonderful?
I think .... with me but .... yet.
Anyway, I ....
I .... to tell you all about it.
Your friend,

....

1 Put the adjectives in the right order.

a red / tasty / apple
.a tasty red apple.
....

3 a young / French /
beautiful / woman
....
....

1 a brown / wooden /
traditional / rocking chair
....
....

4 a(n) expensive / new /
red / shirt
....
....

2 a vase / blue /
glass / modern
....
....

5 a (n) elegant / coat /
long / brown
....
....

2 Put the adjectives in brackets into the correct form adding any necessary words.

Tom's

price :	£15,000
speed:	110 mph
size:	medium
petrol consumption: average
made in 2001

John's

price :	£7,000
speed:	90 mph
size:	small
petrol consumption: low
made in 1987

Carol's

price :	£19,000
speed:	130 mph
size:	large
petrol consumption: high
made in 2006

Tom's car is 1) ...*more expensive than*... John's car (**expensive**) but Carol's car is
2) .... all (**expensive**). Tom's car isn't as 3) .... Carol's car
(**big**). Carol's car is 4) .... all (**big**). Carol's car is 5) .... all
(**modern**). John's car is 6) .... all (**old**). Tom's car is 7) ....
Carol's car (**economical**) but John's car is 8) .... all (**economical**). John's car
isn't as 9) .... Tom's car (**fast**). It is 10) .... Tom's car (**slow**).
Carol's car is 11) .... all (**fast**) but it is 12) .... all (**economical**).

3 **Rewrite the sentences using *too* and *enough*.**

1 Bill plays the violin very well. He can win the competition.

.*Bill plays the violin well enough*.
.*to win the competition*............

2 Rania is tired. She can't continue working.

....
....

3 They have money. They can buy the house.

....
....

4 It's very late. We can't play outside.

....
....

5 Stella is short. She can't be a model.

....
....

6 Pierre is tall. He can reach the top shelf.

....
....

7 We aren't going to the party yet. It's early.

....
....

8 I have five eggs. I can make a cake.

....
....

4 **Put the verbs in brackets into the *present simple*, the *present continuous* or *will*.**

John: Hello, Gary. Where 1) .*are you going*.. **(you/go)**?

Gary: To the sports centre. I've got football practice. Our team 2) .... **(go)** to France next week.

John: Oh, that 3) .... **(be)** great! How 4) .... **(you/get)** there?

Gary: We 5) .... **(travel)** by ferry. It 6) .... **(leave)** at 5 o'clock on Wednesday morning.

John: How long 7) .... **(you/stay)** in France?

Gary: For about a week. We 8) .... **(have)** four games to play. The first one 9) .... **(start)** at 3 o'clock on Wednesday afternoon and the last one 10) .... **(finish)** at 5 o'clock the following Tuesday.

John: Do you think you 11) .... **(win)**?

Gary: Of course. Well, I have to go now. The coach 12) .... **(get)** angry if I'm late for training. I 13) .... **(tell)** you all about it when I 14) .... **(get)** back.

5 Put the verbs in brackets into the *present simple*, the *present continuous*, *will*, *be going to* or the *future continuous*.

1 A: I'm going to the gym this afternoon.
   B: Well, while you .. *are* . **(be)** there,
      I .... **(go)** shopping.

2 A: .... **(you/do)**
      anything special tonight?
   B: I .... **(see)**
      Roger. Would you like to come?

3 A: Look at the sky! It .... **(rain)**.
   B: I .... **(take)** an umbrella with me.

4 A: Lisa, I'm so happy! I got the job!
   B: Wonderful! I .... **(tell)**
      Mum and Dad the good news.

5 A: Are you nervous about the interview, Larry?
   B: Yes. This time tomorrow, I ....
      .... **(talk)** to the company director.

6 A: Where are you going?
   B: I ....
      .... **(get)** some vegetables from the
      supermarket.

7 A: As soon as Mark ....
      .... **(come)** back, tell him to call me.
   B: OK, John.

8 A: Are you looking forward to your holiday?
   B: Oh, yes. This time next week, I ....
      .... **(swim)** in the sea.

6 🎧12 Listen to Wendy telling Eric why he won't be able to have a party next Saturday. What are their friends planning to do? For questions 1–5, write a letter (A–H) next to each person. You will hear the conversation twice.

People			Plans
0	C	Tom	A watch hockey game
1		Jody	B go to London
2		Nick	C go camping
3		Greg	D play in a band
4		Sam	E get married
5		Alan	F visit grandparents
			G play in a football match
			H see a concert

Present Perfect Continuous

🎧 **13** **Listen and repeat. Then act out.**

Form: has / has been + verb -ing

Affirmative	Interrogative	Negative
I have been working	Have I been working?	I have not been working
You have been working	Have you been working?	You have not been working
He has been working	Has he been working?	He has not been working
She has been working	Has she been working?	She has not been working
It has been working	Has it been working?	It has not been working
We have been working	Have we been working?	We have not been working
You have been working	Have you been working?	You have not been working
They have been working	Have they been working?	They have not been working
Short form	**Negative-Interrogative**	**Short form**
I've been working ...	Haven't you been working? ...	I haven't been working ...

---

1 **Fill in the *present perfect continuous* of the verbs in brackets.**

1 He *has been playing* **(play)** football with his friends all afternoon.

2 They .... **(watch)** a comedy for over an hour.

3 Annie .... **(do)** her homework since 10 o'clock this morning.

4 How long .... **(he/work)** as a doctor?

5 The children .... **(study)** since breakfast.

6 We .... **(think)** of buying a house since last year.

7 .... **(you/feel)** ill for a long time?

8 Chris .... **(try)** to fix the motorbike since Tuesday.

Present Perfect Continuous is used:

- for actions which started in the past and continue up to the present.

They **have been making biscuits** since 11 o'clock. (They're still making biscuits.)

- for past actions of certain duration which have visible results or effects, in the present.

Bob is very tired. He **has been working** all day long.

- to express irritation, anger, annoyance, explanation or criticism.

Who **has been reading** my business papers? (showing anger)

- to put emphasis on duration, usually with **for, since** or **how long.**
I've **been typing** letters **since** 9 o'clock.

Present Perfect is used:

- for actions recently completed.

They **have made** a lot of biscuits.
(The biscuits are on the plate, so the action has finished.)

- for actions which happened at an unstated time.

James **has bought** a new car.

- to express personal experiences or changes which have happened.

I've **lost** a lot of weight.

- to put emphasis on number.
I've only **typed three** letters since 9 o'clock.

Note

With the verbs live, feel and work we can use either Present Perfect or Present Perfect Continuous with no difference in meaning.
I've **been living** in London for a year.
or I've **lived** in London for a year.

Non-continuous verbs are not used in Present Perfect Continuous (know, believe, see, like, love, taste, understand, want, etc.)
I've **known** her since 2002.
(NOT: I've been knowing her since 2002.)

Time adverbs used with Present Perfect Continuous:	Time adverbs and expressions used with Present Perfect:
for, since, how long	just, ever, never, always, already, yet, for, since, so far, how long, recently, today, this week / month / year, once, etc.

2 Identify the speech situations, then complete the sentences by putting the verbs in brackets into the *present perfect* or the *present present continuous*.

recently completed action unstated time	anger or annoyance emphasis on duration	personal experience ~~visible results~~

1 .... *visible results* ....

He ... *has been painting* ... (paint) his room.

2 ....

She ....
.... (just/win) the race.

3 ....

.... (you/read) my emails again?

4 ....

They ....
.... (plant) trees since morning.

5 ....

He ....
.... (try) skiing.

6 ....

They ....
.... (buy) a pet dog.

3 Put the verbs in brackets into the *present perfect* or the *present perfect continuous*.

- A: My back hurts.
  B: That's because you 1) ..... *have been working* ..... (work) all day.
  A: I know. But at least I 2) .... (finish) with the gardening.

- A: You look tired. What 3) .... (you/do)?
  B: I 4) .... (play) tennis with Evita.
  A: Oh yes. I 5) .... (see) her play before. She's good, isn't she?
  B: Yes, she is. She 6) .... (beat) me five times since the start of summer.

4 **Put the verbs in brackets into the *present perfect* or the *present perfect continuous*.**

Pam: What are you doing, Ben?

Ben: I 1) *'ve been looking through* (**look through**) my old toy box all morning. It brings back lots of memories. Look, I 2) .... (**find**) my old train set!

Pam: You 3) .... (**play**) with those trains for over an hour. I 4) .... (**watch**) you.

Ben: They're great! I 5) .... (**not/have**) so much fun for years. Look at this one!

Pam: Yes, Ben – it's a very nice train. But 6) .... (**you/see**) the time?

Ben: No... Why?

Pam: It's 10:30 am. Your boss 7) .... (**just/phone**) from the office.

Ben: What for?

Pam: He 8) .... (**wait**) for you all morning. You have an important meeting.

Ben: Oh no! I lost track of time!

5 **Write one word for each space.**

Dear Jessica,

How 1) ..... *are* .... things? I'm sorry that I haven't sent you an email but I've been really busy lately.

For the last two days, I have 2) .... organising a surprise party for my best friend, Sally. I have 3) .... decorated the house with balloons and coloured lights. I still have so many things to do but luckily, Sophie and Pat have been helping with the preparations.

So far, Sophie 4) .... invited all our friends 5) .... Pat has bought Sally's present but we haven't ordered a cake or bought any snacks and soft drinks 6) .... Anyway, we've got plenty of time till Saturday. I'm sure everything 7) .... be fine.

8) .... have you been doing lately? Have you decided 9) .... you'll visit us? I hope you can come during the summer holidays. I do miss you.

Write soon. I can't wait 10) .... hear all your news.

Love,

Pamela

6 Write sentences about yourself. Use the *present perfect* or the *present perfect continuous*.

1 not play basketball for ...

. I haven't played basketball for...
. a week.....................

2 listen to music since ... .
....

3 know my best friend for ... .
....

4 live here for ... .
....

5 not see my friends since ... .
....

Speaking Activity

(Talking about things you have already done or haven't done yet)

Work in pairs. Ask and answer questions as in the example:

tired – clean / house	excited – plan / party	dirty – work / garden
• make / beds (✓)	• send / invitations (✓)	• plant / tomatoes (✓)
• clean / windows (✓)	• put up / decorations(✓)	• cut / grass(✓)
• mop / floors (✗)	• order / cake (✗)	• water / plants (✗)
• hoover / carpets (✗)	• sort out / music to play (✗)	• pick / flowers (✗)

A: You look tired. What have you been doing?

B: I've been cleaning the house.

A: What have you done so far?

B: Well, I've made the beds and cleaned the windows but I haven't mopped the floors or hoovered the carpets yet, etc.

Writing Activity

Write a letter to your pen friend telling him/her about the party you are planning.

Dear .... ,

How are you? I am so excited. For the last week, I .... a
.... party for .... It's going to be a big surprise!

Since yesterday, I .... and ....

It is a lot of work but my .... me. So far, we

.... but we .... yet.

Well, that's all for now. Write back soon.

Love,

....

Past Continuous – Was going to – Used to – Be/Get used to

 Listen and repeat. Then act out.

Past Continuous: **was/were + verb -ing**

Affirmative	Interrogative	Negative	
		Long form	**Short form**
I was helping	Was I helping?	I was not helping	I wasn't helping
You were helping	Were you helping?	You were not helping	You weren't helping
He was helping	Was he helping?	He was not helping	He wasn't helping etc.
She was helping	Was she helping?	She was not helping	
It was helping	Was it helping?	It was not helping	**Negative - Interrogative**
We were helping	Were we helping?	We were not helping	
You were helping	Were you helping?	You were not helping	Wasn't I helping?
They were helping	Were they helping?	They were not helping	Weren't you helping? etc.

Time words used with the Past Continuous: while, when, as

1 **The fire alarm went off at the Crown Hotel last night. Put the verbs in the *past continuous* to describe what each person was doing.**

1 When the fire alarm went off, Mr Cook .... *was talking* .... **(talk)** on the phone.

2 A porter .... **(carry)** some luggage.

3 Miss Jones .... **(read)** a magazine.

4 Two men .... **(sit)** in the reception area.

Past Continuous versus Past Simple

| **Past Continuous is used:** | **Past Simple is used:** |

Past Continuous is used:

- for an action that was in the middle of happening at a stated time in the past.

  At 8 o'clock last night she **was watching** TV.

- for two or more actions which were happening at the same time in the past (simultaneous actions).

  At 5 o'clock yesterday afternoon Ben **was doing** his homework while his dad **was cooking** dinner.

- for a past action which was in progress when another action interrupted it. We use Past Continuous for the interrupted action and Past Simple for the action which interrupts it.

  Linda **was watching** TV when the phone **rang**.

- to describe the background to the events in a story.

  We **were walking** in the woods. It **was raining** hard ...

Past Simple is used:

- for an action completed at a stated time in the past.

  He **finished** his homework at 7 o'clock.

- for actions which happened one after another (sequence of actions).

  He **slipped**,
  fell over and **hurt** his ankle.

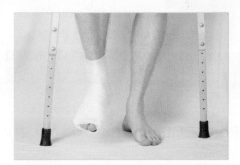

- with non-continuous verbs: appear (=**seem**), believe, belong, cost, feel, forget, hate, have (=**possess**), know, like, love, mean, need, prefer, realise, remember, see, seem, smell, sound, suppose, taste, think, understand, want, etc.

  Sylvia **saw** Alex at the party yesterday.

- for people who are no longer alive.

  Shakespeare **wrote** a lot of plays. (Shakespeare is dead. He won't write any more.)

2 Use the *past continuous* or the *past simple* and the phrases to label the pictures. Then identify the speech situations.

- ~~action in the middle of happening~~
- simultaneous actions
- sequence of actions
- completed action
- interrupted action
- people who are no longer alive

1 .action in the middle. .of happening.........

(they sleep/at 11 o'clock/ yesterday evening)

.They were sleeping.. at 11 o'clock......... yesterday evening...

2 ....

(wash up/feed the dog/an hour ago)

3 ....

(last night/Mrs Smith knit/Mr Smith watch TV)

4 ....

(they sunbathe/start to rain)

5 ....

(Gustave Eiffel/build/the Eiffel Tower)

6 ....

(Claire/have first birthday / 2 days ago)

Was / Were going to

Was going to is used to express fixed arrangements in the past, unfulfilled plans or an action which someone intended to do in the past but didn't do.

He got up early. **He was going to** catch the 6 o'clock train. (fixed arrangement in the past)
She was going to travel around Europe but she didn't because she fell ill. (unfulfilled plan)
She was going to buy a new car but in the end she repaired her old one. (She intended to buy a car but she didn't.)

6 **Past Continuous – Was going to – Used to – Be/Get used to**

3 Write what was going to happen but didn't.

catch / bus	have / picnic	~~buy / dress~~

1 .She.was.going.to... .buy.a.dress.... but a thief stole her bag.

2 .... but he was too late.

3 .... but it started to rain.

4 Put the verbs in brackets into the *past simple* or the *past continuous*. Then say which uses of these tenses are shown in each extract.

A Heath Ledger 1) ...was... **(be)** a very talented Australian actor who 2) .... **(try)** different kinds of roles. One of the last films he 3) .... **(take)** part in was *The Dark Knight*, where he 4) .... **(play)** the evil Joker. Sadly, he 5) .... **(die)** on January 22nd, 2008 at the age of 28.

B It 1) .... **(happen)** at 8 o'clock last night. John and his wife, Jane, 2) .... **(sit)** in their living room. They 3) .... **(watch)** TV while their daughter 4) .... **(play)** with her toys. Suddenly, the room 5) .... **(start)** to shake and two vases 6) .... **(fall)** to the ground.

5 Put the verbs in brackets into the *past simple* or the *past continuous*.

1 A: I .was.walking. **(walk)** home yesterday when I ....ran.into.... **(run into)** Jennifer.
   B: Is she OK? I haven't seen her for such a long time.
2 A: What .... **(happen)** to your leg?
   B: I .... **(break)** it while I .... **(ski)**.
3 A: I .... **(call)** you yesterday morning but you .... **(not/be)** at home.
   B: Yes. I .... **(walk)** my dog.

Used to – Be/Get Used to + noun / pronoun / -ing

Used to **is used to talk about past habits. It has the same form in all persons, singular and plural. It forms its negative and interrogative form with** did.

I **used to** cry when I was a baby.
I **didn't use to** sleep late.
Did you use to sleep late?

Be/Get used to **is used to talk about habitual actions and means 'be/get accustomed to', 'be in the habit of'.**

I'm **not used to getting up** early.
They **are used to cold weather**.
You'**ll get used to her** when you get to know her better.

---

6 **Rewrite Victoria's comments using** *used to* **or** *didn't use to* **as in the example:**

1 *Victoria used to work long hours.*
2 ....
3 ....
4 ....
5 ....
6 ....

7 **Complete the sentences with the correct form of** *used to*, *be/get used to* **and the verbs in brackets.**

1 Lisa is very tired this morning. She .... *isn't used to staying up* .... (**not/stay up**) late.
2 Don't worry. You .... soon .... (**wear**) contact lenses.
3 He .... (**eat**) a lot of chocolate when he was a child.
4 They didn't like living near the airport but they .... it.
5 I .... (**get up**) at 6:30 am, so it doesn't bother me.
6 Sheila lives in the city but she still .... (**not**) all the noise.

8 Put the verbs in brackets into the *past continuous* or the *past simple*.

Last night I 1) ....*had*.... **(have)** a wonderful dream. This is what I 2) .... **(dream)**. We 3) .... **(take)** a trip to Hawaii. I 4) .... **(be)** with my family and two of my friends. We 5) .... **(be)** on a ship and we 6) .... **(travel)** to Honolulu. On the ship there 7) .... **(be)** a party. We 8) .... **(sit)** on nice comfortable seats and we 9) .... **(drink)** exotic juices. Lots of people 10) .... **(dance)** and the music 11) .... **(play)** loudly. We 12) .... **(have)** a lot of fun! When the ship 13) .... **(arrive)** in Honolulu, a man 14) .... **(wait)** to take us to our hotel. The hotel where we 15) .... **(stay)** was by a beach lined with palm trees. Drums 16) .... **(beat)** and people on the beach 17) .... **(sing)** and 18) .... **(dance)** to the music. The music 19) .... **(get)** louder and louder until I 20) .... **(hear)** a ringing sound. It 21) .... **(be)** my alarm clock! It 22) .... **(be)** 7 o'clock and time to get up for school.

9 Circle the mistake (A or B), then correct it.

1 While we <u>were having</u> a picnic, it <u>was starting</u> to rain.
              A   **(B)**   ...*started*...

2 Alicia was painting a picture <u>when</u> her mum <u>was cooking</u>.
                            A   **B** ....

3 Laura <u>was taking off</u> her coat and <u>sat</u> down.
              A   **B** ....

4 While we <u>were</u> on holiday, we <u>were spending</u> most of our time sightseeing.
           A   **B** ....

5 Costas <u>listened</u> to his iPod, so he <u>didn't hear</u> the doorbell ring.
          A   **B** ....

Speaking Activity

(Talking about a bad experience)

Chain story: Look at the pictures. Use the phrases to say what happened to John and his friends.

- John and friends / decide to take walk in the forest
- sun / shine, birds / sing
- they / enjoy walk / when / hear roar
- as they / look around / see big bear / come towards them

- they / try not to panic
- they / quickly / fall to ground / not move at all
- bear / smell / them
- luckily / after few minutes / bear / leave
- they / feel / relieved / be / safe

S1: Last weekend John and his friends decided to take a walk in the forest, etc.

Writing Activity

Now imagine you are John. Write in your diary about the terrifying experience you had.

Dear Diary,

While on holiday, I had the worst experience of my life!

Last Saturday, my friends and I ....

....

....

....

....

....

....

1 Put the verbs in brackets into the *present perfect* or *present perfect continuous*.

1 They ..*have*.. .*bought*....... (buy) a new house.

2 He .... (examine) patients all day.

3 The play .... (just/finish).

4 Mr Phillips ...... (teach) English for twenty years.

5 The baby .... (cry) for two hours.

6 Mrs Robins .... (clean) the house all morning.

7 He .... (do) the shopping.

8 She .... (just/break) the vase.

2 There was a power cut at the library yesterday evening. Look at the picture and put the verbs in the list into the *past continuous* to describe what each person was doing.

look	study	read	~~surf~~	make

1 Mandy ..*was surfing*........ the Net.
2 Mr Taylor .... photocopies.
3 Jill .... for a book.
4 Sam .... a magazine.
5 Tony and Wendy ....

66

3 Put the verbs in brackets into the *past simple* or *past continuous*. Then say which uses of these tenses are shown in each extract.

A Lady Diana Frances Spencer 1) ..*married*.. (marry) Prince Charles in July, 1981. She 2) .... (be) the mother of their two sons, William and Harry.

The British people 3) .... (love) her for her kindness and beauty. Princess Diana 4) .... (care) a lot about the sick and the poor all over the world. Unfortunately, she 5) .... (die) in a car accident on August 31st, 1997.

B One cool and windy afternoon James 1) .... (decide) to go to the park. When he 2) .... (get) there, a girl 3) .... (fly) her kite while several boys 4) .... (play) football. The boys 5) .... (ask) James to play with them. Everyone 6) .... (enjoy) themselves when suddenly dark clouds 7) .... (cover) the sky.

4 Fill in: *used to* or *didn't use to*.

1 I ...*didn't use to*... eat vegetables but I do now.
2 He .... ride a motorbike but he doesn't any more.
3 I .... eat a lot of sweets but I don't any more.
4 She .... like dogs but she has got two now.
5 He .... exercise. He goes jogging every morning now.

5 Complete the sentences with a verb from the list in the correct form.

| watch | go | ~~drive~~ | ride | wash | live |

1 Klaus had to get used to ....*driving*.... on the left.
2 We used to .... in a small town but now we live in London.
3 Lucas used to .... a lot of TV. Now he prefers to listen to music.
4 Little children are used to .... to bed early in the evening.
5 Linda used to .... a motorbike but I think she has a car now.
6 We haven't got a dishwasher, so we're used to .... the dishes by hand.

6 **Choose the correct answer.**

1 We used ...... in a flat but now we live in a big house.
   A live   **B** to live   **C** living

2 I'm used ...... up very early in the morning, so it doesn't bother me.
   A to get   **B** getting   **C** to getting

3 It was difficult at first but Max is getting used ...... on the left.
   A drive   **B** to driving   **C** driving

4 Dad didn't use ...... on Saturdays but he does now.
   A work   **B** working   **C** to work

5 When Helen was little, her father used ...... her stories before going to bed.
   A tell   **B** to tell   **C** telling

6 I never got used ...... German when I lived in Germany. It was difficult for me to learn.
   A to speaking   **B** speaking   **C** speak

7 Neil isn't used ...... Chinese food.
   A to eat   **B** to eating   **C** eating

8 Tom used ...... in Rome but now he's moved back to London.
   A live   **B** to living   **C** to live

Listening

7 **15** **You will hear information about a history museum. Listen and complete questions 1–5. You will hear the information twice.**

Jefferson History Museum

You can see:

Main Floor:
   old *photos* of the town

Upstairs:

   Left: **1** .... people used to use

   Right: **2** .... clothing on display

   Price of guidebook: **3** €...........................

   Closing time: **4** ....

   There are staff members present to answer: **5** your ....

Listen and repeat. Then act out.

Reflexive–Emphatic pronouns	Personal pronouns		Possessive adjectives	Possessive pronouns
	before verbs as subjects	after verbs as objects	followed by nouns	not followed by nouns
myself	I	me	my	mine
yourself	you	you	your	yours
himself	he	him	his	his
herself	she	her	her	hers
itself	it	it	its	–
ourselves	we	us	our	ours
yourselves	you	you	your	yours
themselves	they	them	their	theirs

Reflexive Pronouns are used:

after certain verbs (cut, behave, burn, enjoy, hurt, look at, teach, etc.) when the subject and the object of the verb are the same person.
I've cut **myself**.

Emphatic Pronouns are used:

at the end of the sentence or after the noun phrase they refer to to emphasise the noun or the fact that one person and not another performs an action.
He can fix the car (by) **himself**.

Note these expressions: Enjoy yourself! = Have a good time! Behave yourself! = Be good!
I like being by myself. = I like being alone. She lives by herself. = She lives alone.
Help yourself to tea. = Don't wait to be offered tea.

7 Reflexive – Emphatic Pronouns / Both – Neither / Possessives

Note the difference: -selves / each other

They are looking at **themselves** in the mirror.

They are looking at **each other**.

1 **Write sentences as in the example:**

1 A: What is he doing?

B: He .... *is teaching* .... **(teach)**
.. *himself* .. how to play the piano.

2 A: What did she do?

B: She .... **(hurt)**
.... while she was

playing in the garden.

3 A: What are they doing?

B: They ....

(enjoy) .... at a party.

4 A: What has he done?

B: He ....

(bake) some bread ....

5 A: What do they often do?

B: They ....

(make) pies ....

6 A: What are you doing?

B: I ....

(paint) this picture ....

2 **Fill in:** *myself, yourself, himself, ourselves* **or** *yourselves*.

Jim: Bye Mum. We're going to Simon's birthday party.

Mum: OK. Enjoy 1) ...*yourselves*... boys. And Jim, don't eat too much cake or you'll make

2) .... sick. Did you get him a card?

Jim: Yes, we did. Actually, Mark and I made it 3) .... What are you and Dad going to do this afternoon, Mum?

Mum: I'm going to buy 4) .... some new clothes and Dad's going to study. He's trying to teach 5) .... Italian. Have a good time at the party but behave 6) ....

3 **Fill in the appropriate** *reflexive pronoun* **or** *each other*.

1 A: Did you help Jimmy finish his homework?

  B: No, he finished it ..... *himself* ....

  ....

2 A: What's wrong with Tom and Henry?

  B: They don't get along with ....

  ....

3 A: Are you going to the park with your friends?

  B: No, they are going by ....

4 A: How is Dan?

  B: I don't know. We haven't seen

  .... for a long time.

5 A: I'm hungry. Have you got anything to eat?

  B: There is some food in the fridge. Help

  .... !

6 A: Do you need to turn off the heater?

  B: No, it will actually turn ....

  off.

Possessive case with 's / s'	Possessive case with of
1 singular nouns + 's (person or animal) the boy**'s** bag, the cat**'s** head **2 regular plural nouns + '** the boy**s'** bags **3 irregular plural nouns not ending in s/-es + 's** the children**'s** toys	**1 of + name of a thing** the banks **of** the river **2 of + possessive case/possessive pronoun** That's a friend **of Mary's** (= one of Mary's friends). I've got a book **of yours** (= one of your books).

Note: **phrase of place + 's:**   at the chemist**'s**   = at the chemist's shop

  phrase of time + 's / ': today**'s** paper   = the paper that has come out today

  two week**s'** holiday = a holiday that lasts for two weeks

7 Reflexive – Emphatic Pronouns / Both – Neither / Possessives

4 Connect the nouns using -'s, -' or ... of ... .

1 bike / Mary ..... *Mary's bike* .....
2 news / today ....
3 top / stairs ....

4 CDs / girls ....
5 hat / Juan ....
6 books / students ....

5 Rewrite the sentences using the correct possessive form.

1 Julie is – **at chemist** – **shop** .. *Julie is at the chemist's.*..
2 Avril looks after – **her neighbour** – **children** ....
3 Helen always listens to – **her friends** – **the advice** ....
4 Are you going to – **Lucy** – **the party**? ....
5 That girl over there is – **a friend** – **my** ....

6 Fill in the correct *subject* / *object* / *possessive pronouns* or *adjectives*.

Last year Francis and 1) ...*his*... sister Caroline went on holiday to New York. Unfortunately, 2) .... was a disaster. First of all, 3) .... nearly missed 4) .... flight because 5) .... car broke down. Then Francis couldn't find 6) .... ticket, until Caroline realised that she had both 7) .... ticket and 8) .... in 9) .... handbag. When 10) .... got to New York, 11) .... couldn't find 12) .... hotel. Caroline fell over and twisted 13) .... ankle when 14) .... got out of the taxi. Francis tried to help 15) .... but strained 16) .... back, so 17) .... both had to spend the rest of the week in bed. This year 18) .... are hoping to see some of the sights of New York on 19) .... holiday.

Some / Any / No

	Positive	Interrogative	Negative
	some	**any**	**no/not any**
people	someone somebody	anyone anybody	no one (not anyone) nobody (not anybody)
things	something	anything	nothing (not anything)
place	somewhere	anywhere	nowhere (not anywhere)

7 Fill in: *some, any, no* or their derivatives.

When the three bears came home, Mother Bear said, "1) .....*Some*.... of the soup has gone!" The little bear looked in his bowl and said, "There is 2) .... soup in my bowl! There isn't 3) .... left at all! 4) .... has eaten it!" Then the bears heard 5) .... in the bedroom. Father Bear called out, "Is there 6) .... there?" but 7) .... answered. The little girl in the bedroom woke up and looked for 8) .... to hide but she couldn't find 9) .... Father Bear called out again, "Is there 10) .... there?" and the frightened girl said, "No, 11) .... is here!"

8 Fill in the gaps with the words given.

anything   someone   some   anywhere
something   nobody   ~~nowhere~~   any

1 A: Do you like living in Switzerland?
   B: It's OK. But .....*nowhere*..... is better than LA.

2 A: I went to Angela's house but there was .... there.
   B: They have gone away for the weekend.

3 A: Tina, I need .... help with this project.
   B: Sure, what can I do for you?

4 A: Have you seen Frank ....?
   B: He was in Mr Smith's office two minutes ago.

5 A: I'd like to see you now. I have .... to say to you.
   B: Of course. Come to my office.

6 A: Is .... wrong with Jimmy? He looks upset.
   B: He had an argument with his parents.

7 A: There aren't .... oranges left. Would you like an apple?
   B: No, thanks. I don't like apples.

8 A: Mum, there's .... waiting for you at the door.
   B: Who is it?

7   Reflexive — Emphatic Pronouns / Both — Neither / Possessives

Both — Neither — None — All

Both refers to two people or things. It has a positive meaning and takes a verb in the plural.
Tom is rich. Laura is rich, too.
Both of them **are** rich. **or** They are **both** rich.
All refers to more than two people or things. It has a positive meaning and takes a verb in the plural.
John, Mary and Kevin are students. **All of** them **are** students. **or** They are **all** students.

Neither refers to two people or things. It has a negative meaning and takes a verb either in the singular or the plural.
Tom isn't poor. Laura isn't poor either.
Neither of them **is / are** poor.
None refers to more than two people or things. It has a negative meaning and takes a verb either in the singular or the plural.
John, Mary and Kevin haven't got a car.
None of them **has / have** a car.

---

9   Use *both*, *neither*, *none* or *all* and write sentences as in the example:

1   Katy can ride a bicycle. Sue can ride a bicycle, too. *Both of them can ride a bicycle.* or *They can both ride a bicycle.*

2   Matias doesn't like fish. Greg doesn't like fish either.

. . . .
. . . .
. . . .

3   Mr Tibbs doesn't drive carefully. Mr Smith doesn't drive carefully either.

. . . .
. . . .
. . . .

4   Laura, Sally and Moira are running.

. . . .
. . . .
. . . .

5   Ted has won a medal. Tony has won a medal, too.

. . . .
. . . .
. . . .

Quelle heure est-il?

6   Bob, Nick and Carlos don't speak French.

. . . .
. . . .
. . . .

10 Circle the correct item.

1 A: How did your class do in the exam?
   B: Luckily, we .... passed.
   A neither   **B** both   **C** all

2 A: Did you find someone to watch the boys?
   B: No. I saw two babysitters yesterday but .... of them had much experience.
   A both   **B** all   **C** neither

3 A: Are the girls going shopping with you?
   B: No, ... of them are coming. They've made other plans.
   A none   **B** all   **C** both

4 A: How many sisters do you have?
   B: Two and .... of them are younger than me.
   A none   **B** both   **C** all

5 A: How will you get to the party?
   B: I'll probably ask my dad to give me a lift. .... of my friends have a car.
   A None   **B** All   **C** Both

6 A: Both of these dresses look lovely.
   B: Yes, but I think .... of them fits me well.
   A all   **B** none   **C** neither

7 A: Who do you like better, Christina Aguilera or Britney Spears?
   B: I don't have a favourite. I think they are .... great singers.
   A neither   **B** both   **C** all

8 A: There are some very nice clothes in that shop.
   B: Yes, I know but .... of them are very expensive.
   A both   **B** all   **C** none

9 A: Are you going to town today?
   B: Yes, I want to return the two vases I bought yesterday because they are .... damaged.
   A neither   **B** both   **C** all

Another, Other, The other, The second

- **We use another in front of singular countable nouns to mean 'one more' or 'a different one'.**
  I don't like this shirt. I'm going to buy **another** one.

- **We use other in front of plural nouns when we refer to 'different ones'.**
  Jim likes travelling and learning about **other** cultures.

- **We use the other in front of singular and plural countable nouns. It means 'not this one' or 'the remaining one(s)'.**
  The police arrested one man but **the other** one got away.
  Where are **the other** books?

- **We use the other when there are two and the second when we list things in order and there are more than two.**
  The first test was easy, **the second** was OK but the third was very difficult.

7 Reflexive – Emphatic Pronouns / Both – Neither / Possessives

11 Fill in the gaps with *another*, *(the) other*, or *(the) second*.

1 He asked the coach to give him ...*another*.... chance.

2 This ring is gold but .... one is silver.

3 Amy has got three boys. The first one is sixteen, ... one is nine and the third is four.

4 There are .... ways to get to the town centre but this is the quickest.

5 Helen is much cleverer than all .... students in her class.

6 Her first novel wasn't good, her .... one was OK but her third was excellent.

Speaking Activity

(Finding similarities and differences)

Imagine your parents are leaving you alone for the weekend. In pairs, say what you can/can't do by yourself. Use the phrases in the list.

- make breakfast
- cook dinner
- do homework
- tidy room
- iron clothes
- do washing-up
- wash clothes
- cut grass
- clean house

A: I can make breakfast by myself.

B: I can't cook dinner by myself, etc.

Writing Activity

Write a short paragraph about what you and your sister / brother can / can't do by yourselves when your parents aren't home. Stick pictures.

I can make breakfast and wash the dishes by myself. My sister / brother ....

....

....

....

....

....

....

Past Perfect

Listen and repeat. Then act out.

Past Perfect: had + past participle

Affirmative		Negative	
Long form	**Short form**	**Long form**	**Short form**
I had waited	I'd waited	I had not waited	I hadn't waited
You had waited	You'd waited	You had not waited	You hadn't waited
He had waited	He'd waited	He had not waited	He hadn't waited
She had waited	She'd waited	She had not waited	She hadn't waited
It had waited	It'd waited	It had not waited	It hadn't waited
We had waited	We'd waited	We had not waited	We hadn't waited
You had waited	You'd waited	You had not waited	You hadn't waited
They had waited	They'd waited	They had not waited	They hadn't waited

Interrogative	Short answers
Had I waited?	**Had** I/you/he/she/it/we/you/they eaten lunch?
Had you waited?	Yes, I/you/he/she/it/we/you/they **had**.
Had he waited?	No, I/you/he/she/it/we/you/they **hadn't**.
Had she waited? etc	

Past Perfect **is used:**

- **for a past action which happened** before **another** past action **or** before **a stated past time.**
  She **had already left** when I got home. She **had arrived** by 8 o'clock.

- **for an action which finished in the past and whose result was visible in the past.**
  He was happy. He **had won** the race.

- **as the past equivalent of Present Perfect.**
  She **isn't** in her office. She **has already left**. (before a present time)
  She **wasn't** in her office. She **had already left**. (before a past time)

Time expressions used with Past Perfect
before, after, just, yet, already, for, since, ever, never, till / until, when, by, by the time, etc.

8 Past Perfect

1 Put the verbs in brackets into the correct form of the *past perfect* as in the example:

1 The students left the classroom because the bell ..... *had rung* ..... **(ring)**.

2 Rick .... **(not/finish)** the report by the time his boss returned.

3 After they .... **(put up)** their tents, they made a fire.

4 The fans were excited because their team .... **(win)**.

5 .... the burglars .... **(get away)** by the time the police arrived?

6 After Jane .... **(finish)** studying, she went out with some friends.

2 Look at the picture and ask and answer questions as in the example:

Last night the Dicksons had a birthday party for their daughter, Sally. What had they done and what hadn't they done before they went to bed?

1 **(Sally / open / all her presents)** *Had Sally opened all her presents? Yes, she had.*

2 **(they / drink / all the lemonade)** ....

3 **(they / eat / all the cake)** ....

4 **(Mum / let / cat in)** ....

5 **(they / eat / all the sandwiches)** ....

6 **(they / tidy / the room)** ....

3 Fill in the *present perfect* or the *past perfect*.

1 They ....*had done*.... **(do)** their homework before they went to the park.

2 They are out of the supermarket. They .... **(do)** their shopping.

3 He can't pay the bill. He .... **(lose)** his wallet.

4 He bought a car after he .... **(save)** enough money.

5 She signed the letter after she .... **(write)** it.

6 Her hair is wet. She .... **(wash)** it.

Note the difference:

Past Perfect

When his sister phoned, Tim **had left**.
(Tim had left before his sister phoned.)

Past Simple

When his sister phoned, Tim **left**.
(His sister phoned and then Tim left.)

8 Past Perfect

4 Fill in the *past simple* or the *past perfect*, then state which action happened first.

1 When I .... *arrived* .... **(arrive)** at the station, the train ... *had left* ... **(leave)**. first action: ... *had left* ...

2 We .... **(light)** the candles because the lights .... **(go off)**. first action: ....

3 When I got home I .... **(discover)** that somebody .... **(break into)** my flat. first action: ....

4 The patient .... **(die)** before the ambulance .... **(reach)** the hospital. first action: ....

5 Billy .... **(eat)** all the cakes by the time the other children .... **(arrive)** at the party. first action: ....

5 Put the verbs in brackets into the *past perfect* or the *past simple*.

1 Rafael .... *lit* .... **(light)** the candles when she arrived.

2 Rafael .... **(light)** the candles when she arrived.

3 When she arrived at the theatre, he .... **(buy)** the tickets.

4 When she arrived at the theatre, he .... **(buy)** the tickets.

5 When he came home, they .... **(have)** dinner together.

6 When he came home, she .... **(already/have)** dinner.

6 **Use the ideas to make sentences as in the example:**

- Nancy / make a wish − blow out the candles
- He / put on his winter coat − go outside
- Artemis / watch her favourite programme − turn off the TV
- The boys / play rugby − ride their bikes home
- Mr Newton / pack his bags − take taxi to the airport
- They / save enough money − buy a house

After Nancy had made a wish, she blew out the candles.
Before Nancy blew out the candles, she had made a wish.

7 **Complete the sentences using the *past perfect*. Use the verbs in the list.**

pass	~~finish~~	tidy	leave	lose	start

1 I watched TV after I *had finished my homework* .
2 It began to rain after I ....
3 My best friend was excited because he ....
4 By the time my mum got home, I ....
5 When I walked into the classroom, ...
6 I was sad because I ....

8 **Put the verbs in brackets into the *past perfect* or the *past simple*.**

Jessica 1) .... *looked* .... (look) at her watch. It 2) .... (be) already 10:30 at night. She 3) .... (spend) all day writing her article, so it was no surprise she 4) .... (feel) so exhausted. Jessica 5) .... (stand up) and 6) .... (look) out the window. The street lights 7) .... (be) on and the rain 8) .... (stop). She 9) .... (not/be) out all day, so she 10) .... (decide) to take a drive. Jessica 11) .... (feel) happy and relaxed. She 12) .... (finally/finish) her article for the magazine. It 13) .... (take) her all weekend.

Speaking Activity

(Talking about actions that happened before another action in the past)

Look at the pictures. Prepare a short story. Use the ideas to help you.

- Lucy and Jane / want / go to concert / last Saturday
- they / buy tickets / a month before
- Lucy's brother / promise / drive there
- they / get stuck / traffic / because / accident happen
- they / take train
- when / they arrive / concert finish
- Lucy / be very sad

S1: Lucy and Jane wanted to go to Beyoncé's concert last Saturday.

S2: They had bought their tickets a month before, etc.

Writing Activity

Imagine you are Lucy. Use the information from the Speaking Activity to write a story adding any necessary linkers.

Last Saturday was the worst night of my life! My friend Jane and I . . . .

. . . .

. . . .

. . . .

. . . .

. . . .

. . . .

. . . .

1 **Fill in the correct reflexive pronouns.**

When Jane woke up on Monday, she saw the note she had written to 1) ....*herself*.... so she would remember to visit her boss in the hospital. He'd fallen off a ladder and hurt 2) .... quite badly. She knew her children could dress and feed 3) ...., so she got dressed and left immediately. She drove to the hospital, got out of the car and shut the door. Then she saw the keys inside. "Oh no, I've locked 4) .... out!" she said to 5) .... She knew it was the start of a terrible day.

2 **Underline the correct item.**

1 The **chair's leg** / <u>**leg of the chair**</u> is broken.
2 These are the **childrens' books** / **children's books**.
3 They went for **a two weeks' holiday** / **a holiday of two weeks** in France.
4 I've got a CD of **your** / **yours**.
5 Mum isn't at home. She's gone to the **butcher's** / **butcher**.
6 Layla is a friend of my **sister** / **sister's**.
7 Where is **the newspaper of today** / **today's newspaper**?

3 **Choose the correct item.**

1 There is ...... in the box. It's empty.
  (A) nothing   **B** something   **C** anything

2 I don't want to go ...... tonight. Let's stay at home.
  A somewhere **B** anywhere   **C** nowhere

3 Ken and Robert are my older brothers. ...... them can drive a car.
  A Neither   **B** All of   **C** Both of

4 Is there ...... milk in the fridge?
  A some   **B** any   **C** no

5 I rang the bell but there was ...... answer.
  A no   **B** any   **C** some

6 Is Mrs Williams here? I want to ask her ....
  A anything   **B** nothing   **C** something

7 Cathy has a lot of friends. ...... them live in London.
  A Both of   **B** All of   **C** None

8 Bob, Nick and Michael are doctors. ...... them is a teacher.
  A None of   **B** Neither of   **C** All of

9 There isn't ...... in the shop. It's closed.
  A anybody   **B** nobody   **C** somebody

4 **Put the verbs in brackets into the *past perfect* or the *past simple*.**

A James 1) ....*wanted*.... **(want)** to go on a business trip to Italy last week. When he
2) .... **(get)** to the airport, he 3) ....
(realise) he 4) .... **(forget)** his passport at home. So, he
5) .... **(go)** back home to get it but when he
6) .... **(arrive)** at the airport, his plane 7) ....
(already/leave).

B Billy 1) .... **(not/relax)** all week. It 2) ....
(be) almost 9 o'clock on Friday morning and his Maths exam 3) ....
(be) about to begin. He 4) .... **(study)** hard but he
5) .... **(feel)** really nervous.

5 **Look at the table and answer the questions.**

	Tom, 15	Akira, 16	Harry, 13
Lives in	London	Tokyo	Sheffield
Likes	Maths	Art	Science
Sports	cricket	football	tennis
Enjoys	chess, walking	going to cinema	playing guitar, walking
Family	1 sister	2 brothers, 1 sister	1 sister
Ambition	become a teacher	become a pilot	become a doctor

1 Who lives in Newcastle? ...*None of them live(s) in Newcastle.*...
2 Who likes History? ....
3 Who enjoys walking, Tom or Harry? ....
4 Who wants to be an artist? ....
5 Who is over twenty? ....
6 Who plays a sport? ....
7 Who has a sister? ....
8 Who wears glasses, Tom or Akira? ....
9 Who has a brother, Tom or Harry? ....
10 Who has got brown hair, Akira or Harry? ....

6 **Fill in the gaps with *some*, *any*, *no* or one of their compounds.**

1 A: I'm hungry, Mum. I want to eat
     .

   B: Well, there's some fruit on the table.

2 A: Hurry up, Sarah. There's
    . . . . time to waste.
    Your aunt Becky will be here any minute.

   B: Don't worry, Dad. I'm almost ready.

3 A: What's the matter, Larry?

   B: There's . . . . in my
    eye, Mum. It hurts.

4 A: Are you going . . . .
    this weekend?

   B: Yes, I'm going camping with my friends.

5 A: Who gave you this gift?

   B: . . . . at work.

6 A: Is there . . . . good
    on TV tonight?

   B: Yes, the American Music Awards are on
    Channel 8 at 9:00 pm.

7 **Listen and tick (✓) the correct box.**

0 What subject did Karl fail?

A	✓	B		C	

3 Which animal did Annie like most?

A		B		C	

1 Where was Tom's magazine?

A		B		C	

4 Where will Sam leave Ann's MP3 player?

A		B		C	

2 What time did Jane leave home?

A		B		C	

5 Which is Betty's friend?

A		B		C	

9 Functions of Modal Verbs

19 **Listen and repeat. Then act out.**

The modal verbs are: can, could, must, will, would, shall, should, may, might, ought (to), etc. They have the same form in all persons. They come before the subject in questions and take **not** after them in negations. They take an **infinitive without to** after them except for *ought* which is followed by a *to infinitive*.

Can she play tennis? No, she **can't play** tennis but she **can play** golf.

He **ought to listen** to you.

We express ability with:

can (ability in the present or future) **Can** you swim? No, **I can't**. **I can** run fast though.

could / was able to (ability in the past for repeated actions)

She **could / was able to** dance for hours when she was young. (repeated action)

was able to (= managed to) (ability in the past for repeated actions or a single action)

He **was able to** win the race. (single action) (**NOT** ~~He could win the race.~~)

BUT: I couldn't / wasn't able to find my keys. (single action)

He **couldn't / wasn't able to** ski when he was young. (repeated action)

Can is the Present Simple form and could is the Past Simple. Can borrows the rest of its tenses from the verb phrase be able to. She hasn't been able to finish it yet.

---

1 **Fill in: *can, could* or *be able to* in the correct tense.**

John: 1) ...*Can*... you ski?

Dave: Yes, I 2) .... I went skiing last year and I
3) .... go down the learner's slope easily.

John: I 4) .... ski when I was younger but since I hurt my leg I 5) .... (not).

Dave: Actually, I think ice-skating is much easier. I 6) .... ice-skate when I was five years old.

John: Really? I tried ice-skating once but I 7) .... (not) stand up at all!

2 Fill in: *can / can't, could / couldn't, was / wasn't able to* or *have been able to*.

1 A: I'd like to speak to Mr Turner, please.

B: I'm sorry but Mr Turner .... *can't* .... come to the phone right now. He's busy.

2 A: I .... ride a bicycle until I was ten.

B: Well, I didn't learn until I was twelve.

3 A: How was the test, Lily?

B: It was difficult but I .... answer all the questions.

4 A: Is Kim good at languages?

B: Yes, she .... already speak French, German and Spanish.

5 A: Maksim was a very talented child.

B: I know. He .... play the violin when he was seven.

6 A: .... you swim, Sophie?

B: Of course. I .... swim since I was five.

 Listen and repeat. Then act out.

We express possibility / probability **with:**

- **may** / **might** + **present infinitive** He **may** be back before noon. (It's possible.)
  There **might** be some cheese in the fridge. (It's possible.)
- **could** + **present infinitive** He **could** still be at home. (It's possible.)
- **must** + **present infinitive** They look alike. They **must** be twins. (I think they are twins.)
- **can't** + **present infinitive** You have been sleeping all day. You **can't** be tired. (I don't think it's possible that you are tired.)
- **Can ...?** + **present infinitive** **Can** he still be at work? (Is it possible?)
- **could** / **might** + **perfect infinitive** We **could have had** an accident. (It was possible but it didn't happen.)

Might is the past form of **may**. **Might** can also be used for present situations, too.
There's a lot of traffic. I **might** be a little late for the meeting.

3 You are Auntie Claire. This is part of a letter that a 13-year-old student has sent you. Read it, then write him/her a letter giving your advice. Use *may / might, could, must* or *can't.*

> Dear Auntie Claire,
>   I lied to my parents about my exams. When they found out that I had failed, they became very angry. They shouted at me and made me go to my room. They don't let me go out with my friends now. I can't even watch TV. I feel terrible.
>   Unhappy

Auntie *Claire*

Dear Unhappy,
     You 1) ..*may / might*.. have some problems with your family right now but it 2) .... be that serious. You 3) .... try talking to a friend or a relative. You 4) .... have an aunt or a cousin who can help you. You 5) .... find that discussing the problem with them is better. Your parents 6) .... really be as angry as you think; they 7) .... be upset but they 8) .... realise why you're so unhappy. I suggest you try talking to them again – you 9) .... be surprised.
Good luck,
Auntie Claire

🎧21 **Listen and repeat. Then act out.**

May I see Mr Parson?

I'm sorry, you can't see him. He is busy at the moment.

We express permission with:

(asking for permission)

can (informal)	**Can** I borrow your pen?
could (more polite)	**Could** I borrow your car?
may (formal)	**May** I use your phone?
might (more formal)	**Might** I see your driving licence, please?

(giving / refusing permission)

can (informal, giving permission)	You **can** have one more if you want.
may (formal, giving permission)	You **may** stay a little longer.
mustn't (refusing permission)	You **mustn't** park here.
can't (refusing permission)	You **can't** enter this room.

4 Fill in: *can, may, could, mustn't* or *can't.*

Ramon: Mum, 1) ...*can / may*... I go to the library?

Mother: Of course you 2) ...., Ramon but you 3) .... stay very long.

Ramon: 4) .... I stay until 8 o'clock?

Mother: No, you 5) .... because we're leaving for the cinema at 8:30.

(At the library)

Ramon: 6) .... I look at the latest issue of *Musician* magazine, please?

Librarian: Yes, you 7) .... but remember that you 8) .... take it out of the library.

 Listen and repeat. Then act out.

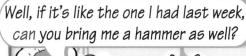

We make requests, offers or suggestions with:

can (request) — **Can** you help me tidy my room?
could / would (polite request) — **Could / Would** you help me with my homework?
could (suggestion) — **Could** we go shopping today?
would you like (polite offer) — **Would you like** some more lemonade?
Shall I / we (suggestion/offer) — **Shall I** post this letter for you? (offer) / **Shall we** buy him a present? (suggestion)

will (offer/request) * for the other uses of 'will' (promises, threats, etc.) see p. 42 — I'll make you some coffee if you want. (friendly offer) / **Will** you do me a favour? (friendly request)

5 Fill in: *can, could, would, shall* or *will.*

John: 1) ....*Would*... you like some more juice, Jane?

Jane: No, thank you. 2) .... we get the bill?

John: OK. Waiter – excuse me, 3) .... you bring us the bill, please?

Waiter: Here you are sir. 4) .... I take these plates away?

John: Yes, please. 5) .... I have a pen to sign this cheque, please? Jane, 6) .... you give me my glasses?

Waiter: 7) .... you like me to get a taxi for you, sir?

John: Yes. Thank you.

Waiter: And I 8) .... bring your coats for you in just a minute.

6   Fill in: *will*, *shall* or *won't*.

Mum: 1) ...*Will*... you be late home tonight, Berta?

Berta: Yes, I 2) .... I'm going to a party. But I 3) .... be too late. I have school tomorrow.

Mum: 4) .... I keep some dinner for you?

Berta: No thanks, Mum. There 5) .... be lots to eat at the party.

Mum: 6) .... I pick you up after the party?

Berta: No, there's no need. I 7) .... come home with Niki and her parents.

Mum: Well, I 8) .... wait up for you.

Berta: No, Mum. Please don't. Oh no! Look at the time! What 9) .... I wear?

 23   **Listen and repeat. Then act out.**

> **We express advice with:**
>
> should / ought to   You **should** walk more. (general advice; I advise you.)
> had better   You**'d better** see your dentist. (advice for a specific situation; it is a good idea.)
>
> **We express criticism with:**
>
> should / ought to + perfect infinitive =   It would have been better if you had ...
>   You **ought to have been** more polite to him. (It was the
>   right thing to do but you didn't do it.)

7   Fill in: *should / ought to* or *had better*.

Jill: You 1) ...*should / ought to*... ask someone to paint your house this year.

Laura: Yes. It's beginning to look a bit dirty. I can't really afford it, though. Do you think I
          2) .... try to get a loan?

Laura: That's a good idea.

Jill: I 3) .... do something about the roof as well. It leaks when it rains.

Laura: Really? You 4) .... take care of it now or the ceiling will fall in!

Jill: Yes, you're right. I 5) .... ring someone today and ask them to look at it.

⑧ **Read the situations and write what you would say using** *should / ought to* **and the correct tense of the infinitive. Use the verbs in the list:**

be	call	lie	~~tell~~	study	eat

1 Frank is the shy, new student at school. You're his only friend and he tells you that an older boy has been bullying him. He is afraid. What do you tell him?

   You ...*should tell the teacher*... .

2 Brenda borrowed her sister's iPod. She wasn't really that careful with it. She put it in her pocket while jogging but it fell out and broke. What do you say to her?

   You ....

3 Your friend loves to eat chips and junk food. Lately, she has put on some weight and doesn't seem to have any energy. What do you tell her?

   You ....

4 You arranged to meet your friend at the shopping centre at 5 o'clock. He shows up at 6 o'clock but he didn't call you to tell you he'd be late. What do you say to him?

   You ....

5 Alma lied to her mother and when her mother found out, she was very upset. What do you say to her?

   You ....

6 Your best friend didn't pass his final exams because he hadn't studied. What do you tell him?

   You ....

We express obligation or necessity with:

must (strong obligation, duty or personal feelings of necessity)

You **must** stop when the traffic light is red.
I **must** see a doctor soon. (I decide it's necessary.)

have to (obligation or external necessity)

I **have to** do my homework every day. (the teachers decide it is necessary – not me)

I've got to (informal; it's necessary)

I**'ve got to** leave early today.

Must is the Present Simple form. It borrows the rest of its tenses from the verb have to. **To form questions and negations of** have to **we use** do/does **(Present Simple) and** did **(Past Simple).**
He **didn't have to** do the shopping yesterday.
You **don't have to** go to school today.
Does he have to be at work on time?

Functions of Modal Verbs

9 **Choose the correct item.**

1 Do you **have to** / **must** wear a uniform at school?

2 I **must** / **have to** work Monday to Friday.

3 Sam usually **has to** / **must** take the rubbish out in the morning.

4 It's cold out. I **must** / **have to** wear my warm coat.

5 How long will you **have to** / **must** stay in the hospital?

6 You **have to** / **must** always obey the school rules.

7 I'm so tired. I **must** / **have to** take a break.

8 My mum says I **must** / **have to** clean my room today.

We express absence of necessity or prohibition with:

mustn't (prohibition)

You **mustn't** feed the animals in the zoo. (It's forbidden.)

can't (prohibition)

You **can't** enter the country club without a card. (You are not allowed.)

needn't (it is not necessary)
don't need to / **don't have to**
  (it is not necessary in the present / future)

You **needn't** take an umbrella. It isn't raining.
You **don't need to** / **don't have to** do it now. You can do it later. (It isn't necessary.)

didn't need to / **didn't have to**
  (it was not necessary in the past)

He **didn't need to** / **didn't have to** go to work yesterday because it was Sunday. (It was not necessary.)

---

10 **Look at the museum rules and complete the sentences below using *must*, *mustn't* or *needn't*.**

MUSEUM RULES

- No cameras allowed.
- No food or drinks allowed in the museum.
- Do not leave children alone.
- Not necessary to join a tour group.
- Do not touch works of art.
- No running in the museum.
- Not necessary to see all the displays.
- Do not throw anything on the floor.

1 You ...*mustn't*... use your cameras.

2 You .... bring any food or drinks.

3 You .... stay close to your parents / teachers.

4 You .... join a tour group.

5 You .... touch the works of art.

6 You .... run in the museum.

7 You .... see all the displays.

8 You .... throw your rubbish in the bin.

11 Fill in: *mustn't, needn't* or *can't*.

John, I want you to look after your brother this evening. He 1) ..*can't*.. go out and he 2) .... forget to do all his homework. You 3) .... let him watch TV until he's finished it. He 4) .... watch the film either – it starts very late. He 5) .... have a bath; he had one in the morning. There's a cake on the table but you 6) .... eat it all – leave some for your sister. You 7) .... do the washing-up. I'm going to do it tomorrow. You 8) .... make too much noise. And you 9) .... go to bed without brushing your teeth. But you 10) .... wait up for us. We might be home quite late because we 11) .... leave the party until most of the guests have left.

12 Make sentences as in the example:

You	must mustn't needn't	~~touch~~ buy take pull do be	the washing-up. I did it myself. the cat's tail. ~~those wires~~. your medicine or you won't get better. quiet in the library. any apples. I bought some yesterday.

1 .*You mustn't touch those wires.* ....
2 ....
3 ....
4 ....
5 ....
6 ....

13 Fill in the gaps with *mustn't, needn't, don't need to / don't have to* or *didn't need to / didn't have to*.

1 A: You .*mustn't*. be late for the meeting.
   B: Yes, I know. I have to leave early to get there on time.

2 A: Shall I do the ironing for you?
   B: No, you .... I'll do it later.

3 A: You .... forget to post the invitations.
   B: OK. I'll post them on my way to work.

4 A: Did Robert get a taxi to the airport?
   B: No, he .... Dad gave him a lift.

5 A: You .... buy that book. I can lend you mine.
   B: Thanks a lot, Ann.

6 A: You .... tell anyone what happened!
   B: Don't worry. I won't say a word.

9 **Functions of Modal Verbs**

14 Fill in the correct modal verb and the speech situations as in the example:

1 You ...*shouldn't*... eat so fast. (...*advice*...)

2 I'm an astronaut; I .... wear a uniform. (.........)

3 Take your umbrella; it .... rain. (.........)

4 I .... get up early on Sundays. (.............)

5 You .... play football in the street. (.............)

6 Children .... pay to get in. (.............)

7 .... I come in? (.............)

8 .... I help you with the painting? (..........)

9 .... you please sit down? (..........)

15 Match the signs to the sentences.

1	D	You mustn't talk here.
2		You can eat and sleep here.
3		You can't drive here.
4		You must pay in cash.
5		You shouldn't drop litter.
6		You should walk here.

(A) **ROAD UNDER CONSTRUCTION**

(B) **PLEASE STAY ON PATH**

(C) **NO CHEQUES OR CREDIT CARDS**

(D) SILENCE

(E) **PLEASE PUT LITTER IN THE BIN**

(F) BED AND BREAKFAST

16 Complete the text with suitable modal verbs. There may be more than one answer.

Milton School

You are at: Exams Homepage > Exam Rules

Exam Rules

(a) You 1) ...... *must* ...... bring your student ID card with you to the examination. You 2) .... put it on your desk so that your teacher can see it.

(b) You 3) .... talk during the exam. When you finish your exam, you 4) .... quietly leave the exam room.

(c) You 5) .... use a calculator for the Mathematics section.

(d) You 6) .... be in the exam room at least 10 minutes before the exam starts.

(e) You 7) .... turn off your mobile phone during the exam.

(f) You 8) .... take your books with you into the exam room.

Giving advice

GAME

In teams, use modal verbs to make up sentences for the following situations. Each correct sentence gets 1 point. The team with the most points wins.

- your friend has got a bad cold
- your friend has put on weight
- your brother has got a test tomorrow
- your friend has failed his/her exams
- your sister doesn't feel well today
- your friend's teacher is in hospital

Team A S1: You should see a doctor, etc.

Speaking Activity

(Talking about obligation / prohibition / giving permission)

Look at the signs / drawings. In pairs, make sentences about summer camp rules using *can*, *must* or *mustn't* and the list of verbs / phrases below.

• smoke • visit • keep camp / clean • eat • listen / MP3 players • bring / pets • be quiet

SUMMER CAMP RULES

Visiting Hours
10:00 am - 14:00 pm

A: You mustn't eat in the tents.

B: You must be quiet between 10:30 pm and 7:00 am, etc.

Writing Activity

Look at the summer camp rules in the Speaking Activity. Write the instructions the camp manager gives to the children who are going camping.

Well children, there are a few things I have to tell you. First of all, you mustn't . . . .

. . . .

. . . .

. . . .

. . . .

24 **Listen and repeat. Then act out.**

- **We use do/does to form questions in Present Simple and did to form questions in Past Simple.**
  Does he play the violin?
  Did he go to work yesterday?

- **To form questions with auxiliary verbs (can, be, will, shall, must, etc.) we put the auxiliary verb before the subject.**
  Is he rich? **Has he** got a car?
  Will he marry her?
  Can you fly a helicopter?

- **Wh-questions begin with a question word and follow the above rules (question words: who, where, when, what, why, how, which, etc.)**
  Who is she?
  What did she do last night?
  Why did you come late?

- **Whose is used to ask about possession.**
  "**Whose** shoes are these?" "They're Tom's."
- **Which is used when there is a limited choice.**
  "**Which** car is yours?" "The red one."

- **With verbs which take a preposition, the preposition goes at the end of the question.**
  Who does it belong **to**?
  Who did you go out **with**?

1 **Write questions about the statements using the words in brackets.**

1 I like playing tennis. **(you)**   *Do you like playing tennis?*
2 She goes to parties. **(How often)**   ....
3 They went to London. **(When)**   ....
4 She is crying. **(Why)**   ....
5 Oliver can swim. **(dive)**   ....
6 Ali hasn't arrived yet. **(Who)**   ....
7 He'll do the cleaning. **(washing-up)**   ....

10 Questions – Question Words – Question Tags

We normally use the following question words when asking about:

people	jobs / things animals / actions	place	time	quantity	manner	reason
Who Whose Which (one of)	What Which (one of)	Where	When How long What time How often	How much How many	How	Why

2 Fill in: *who, whose, which, where, how often, what time, why, how much* or *how many*.

1 "..*Whose*.... is this coat?" "Mine."

2 "..................... is Irina's house?" "Next to the bank."

3 "................. does the party start?" "At 8:30."

4 "................. does this cost?" "£25."

5 "................. is your book?" "The red one."

6 "..................... was he late?" "Because he overslept."

7 "..................... does he visit his grandparents?" "Every Monday."

8 "........... is Robert?" "Julie's brother."

9 "..................... eggs do you need?" "Ten."

Subject / Object Questions

- If who, which or what are the subject of the question, we put the verb in the affirmative.

subject   object
Chris helped **Mary.**

Who helped Mary? (not: Who did help Mary?)

- If who, which or what are the object of the question, we put the verb in the interrogative form.

subject   object
Mary helped **George.**

Who did Mary help?

3 Write questions to which the words in bold are the answers.

1 **Sam** met Julie.   *Who met Julie?*

2 Roger spoke to **Jean**.

3 **Ella** phoned Stuart.

4 Jenny will see **Rosie**.

5 Steve has left a message for **Jim**.

6 Ted doesn't like **Sue**.

7 **Pam** will visit Tom.

8 Jim is playing with **Richard**.

4 Fill in: *what*, *how long*, *when*, *how*, *how much*, *how old*, *why* or *where*.

Police officer: Good morning, madam. 1) .....*What*..... can I do for you?

Mrs Lee: Oh, officer, it's my Ned. He's run away from home.

Police officer: 2) .... do you live?

Mrs Lee: At 14 Church Road.

Police officer: 3) .... is your full name?

Mrs Lee: Jennifer Rose Lee.

Police officer: 4) .... did you last see Ned?

Mrs Lee: At 6 o'clock yesterday evening.

Police officer: 5) .... did he seem?
Was he acting strangely?

Mrs Lee: No, not at all. He seemed all right.

Police officer: 6) .... is Ned?

Mrs Lee: He's twelve.

Police officer: 7) .... money did he have?

Mrs Lee: None. 8) .... do you ask?

Police officer: Well, I'm sure he won't be very far away without any money.

Mrs Lee: 9) .... will it take you to find him?

Police officer: I can't say exactly Mrs Lee but I hope we'll find him very soon. Now, can you tell me
10) .... Ned looks like?

Mrs Lee: Certainly. He's got long floppy ears, a short tail and ...

Police officer: What? You mean Ned is your dog!

> **At the Police Station**

5 Write questions to which the words in bold are the answers.

Giant Pandas live **in China**. They are **black and white animals that have round heads, small black ears and short tails**. They sleep **during the night**. They sleep for **about 8 hours**. They always eat **bamboo**. Giant Pandas are about **150 cm tall** and often weigh about **90 kilos**. They can **climb trees**. They live for about **15 years**.

1 ...*Where do giant pandas live?*...   6 ....
2 ....   7 ....
3 ....   8 ....
4 ....   9 ....
5 ....

Question Tags

- Question tags are short questions put at the end of a statement. We use them, not to ask for information but for confirmation of or agreement to our statement.
  He can drive, **can't he**?

- We form question tags with an auxiliary verb and a personal pronoun (I, you, he, it, etc.). A question tag has the same auxiliary verb as in the statement. If there is no auxiliary verb in the statement, we use do, does or did accordingly.
  She **is** sleeping, **isn't** she?
  He **came** too late, **didn't** he?

- A positive statement is followed by a negative question tag and a negative statement by a positive question tag.
  He **likes** apples, **doesn't** he?
  She **doesn't** like apples, **does** she?
  He **never** complains, **does** he?

- If we are sure of what we are asking and we don't expect an answer, the voice goes down (falling intonation). If we are not sure and we expect an answer, the voice goes up (rising intonation).
  She is pretty, isn't she?   (sure)

  She is a journalist, isn't she? (not sure)

Study the following question tags.

1	"I am"	"aren't I?"	I **am** tall, **aren't I**?
2	"I used to"	"didn't I?"	He **used to** drive to work, **didn't he**?
3	Imperative	"will/won't you?"	Please **help** me, **will/won't you**?
4	"Let's"	"shall we?"	**Let's** make a snowman, **shall we**?
5	"Let me/him", etc.	"will/won't you?"	**Let him** come with us, **will you/won't you**?
6	"I have (got)" (=possess)	"haven't I?"	He **has got** a pen, **hasn't he**?
7	"I have" (used idiomatically)	"don't/doesn't/ didn't I?"	He **had** an accident last week, **didn't he**? He **has** lunch at 12:00 pm, **doesn't he**?
8	"There is/are"	"isn't/aren't there?"	**There's** no one here, **is there**? **There are** a few pears left, **aren't there**?

---

6 Add question tags to the following statements.

1 Let me help you, ...*will/won't you*....?

2 Ann called Sam, ...?

3 She won't tell us the truth, ...?

4 Get out, ...?

5 Rosa has got a pet cat, ...?

6 They aren't going to Paris, ...?

7 She can sing well, ...?

8 Paul will do the shopping, ...?

9 He never speaks rudely, ...?

10 Let's clean the room, ...?

11 Mary didn't use to work so late, ...?

12 She has breakfast at 7:30 am, ...?

13 Let her do it, ...?

14 John spoke to Nick, ...?

15 Rania wears glasses, ...?

16 I am early for the meeting, ...?

7 **Add question tags and short answers as in the example:**

1 Ben sits at the back of the class, ...*doesn't he*...? Yes, ..*he does*................ .
2 He's got dark brown hair, ...? No, ... That's Bill.
3 He wears glasses, ...? Yes, ...
4 They talk a lot in class, ...? Yes, ...
5 Christiana's in the same class, ...? Yes, that's right, ...
6 Her parents are British, ...? No, ... They're Irish.

8 **Tick (✓) sure / not sure according to your teacher's intonation.**

	SURE	NOT SURE
1 You can take the train, <u>can't you?</u> ↗	☐	✓
2 He'll bring his sister, won't he?	☐	☐
3 You don't understand the exercise, do you?	☐	☐
4 Your friends won't come tomorrow, will they?	☐	☐
5 They were on the same plane as us, weren't they?	☐	☐
6 We're late, aren't we?	☐	☐
7 They live next door, don't they?	☐	☐
8 She's got beautiful blue eyes, hasn't she?	☐	☐

So - Neither / Nor

- **We use so + auxilary verb + noun/personal pronoun to agree with positive statements.**
  "They're decorating their house this week." **"So are we."** (We are decorating our house, too.)

- **We use neither / nor + auxiliary verb + noun / personal pronoun to agree with negative statements.**
  "Kate doesn't eat meat." **"Neither / Nor do I."** (I don't eat meat either.)

---

9 **Fill in the gaps with *So, Neither / Nor*, the auxiliary verb and the personal pronoun.**

1 A: I've just bought a new car.
   B: ...*So have I*...... . Mine's a Honda.

2 A: I didn't enjoy that film.
   B: .... It was very boring.

3 A: I am going to the funfair on Saturday.
   B: .... Maybe I'll see you there.

4 A: I was sick last week.
   B: .... I had a terrible cold.

5 A: I don't like broccoli.
   B: .... I think it tastes awful.

6 A: I'm looking forward to this trip.
   B: .... I can't wait.

Who is it?

In pairs try to guess who your partner's favourite celebrity is by asking him/her questions.

A: What does he/she do?

B: He's an actor?

A: Where is he from?

B: England?

A: How old is he? etc.

Speaking Activity

(Interview)

Read the information about this famous young actress. Then in pairs, ask and answer questions.

Fact File

- **Name:** Dakota Fanning
- **Job:** actress
- **Born:** February 23rd, 1994
- **Started acting**: age 5
- **Popular films:** *I am Sam*, *Charlotte's Web*, *War of the Worlds*
- **Lives in:** Los Angeles
- **Hobbies:** reading, swimming, playing the violin, collecting dolls

A: Who's Dakota Fanning?

B: She's an American actress. When was she born? etc.

Writing Activity

Imagine you are a reporter interviewing the famous actress from the Speaking Activity. Write the interview.

A: When did you start acting?

B: I started acting when I was five years old.

A: When were you born?

....

....

....

1 **Choose the correct item.**

1 ...... you play the guitar?
   (A) Can   **B** May   **C** Must

2 They live in a huge house and own three cars. They ...... be rich.
   A can't   **B** can   **C** must

3 ...... I help you carry these bags?
   A Will   **B** Shall
   C Would you like

4 You ...... water the plants. I've already watered them.
   A can't   **B** don't need   **C** needn't

5 He had studied hard, so he ...... answer all the questions in the test.
   A is able to   **B** was able to   **C** can

6 You ...... be rude to your parents.
   A mustn't   **B** must   **C** couldn't

7 You ...... to eat more fruit and vegetables if you want to stay healthy.
   A should   **B** had better   **C** ought

8 Sam ...... be at work today. It's Sunday.
   A can't   **B** mustn't   **C** must

9 I ...... read or write when I was four years old.
   A can't   **B** couldn't   **C** wasn't able

10 We ...... to be at the office at 9 o'clock every morning.
   A should   **B** must   **C** have

11 Dad, ... I go to Kelly's party tomorrow?
   A can   **B** might   **C** will

2 **Fill in the correct modal verb as in the example:**

1 _Could_ you type this letter, please?

2 .... I help you with the cooking?

3 What .... you like to drink, Natsumi?

4 You .... always wear your seatbelt when you drive your car.

5 You .... sit with us if you like.

6 .... I play on the computer, Tony?

3 Complete the questions to which the words in bold are the answers as in the example:

This is **Ricky Blair**. He is from **London**, **England**. He is **17 years old** and his birthday is on **February 27th**. He's **a drummer in a band**. His band's name is **New Groove**. There are **three** members in the band, Ricky, Tommy and Russell. Ricky's favourite kind of music is **rock** and his favourite drummer is **Dominic Howard** of the British band **Muse**.

1 .....*Who*..... is this?

2 .... is he from?

3 .... old is he?

4 .... is his birthday?

5 .... does he do?

6 .... is his band's name?

7 .... members are there in the band?

8 .... is his favourite kind of music?

9 .... is his favourite drummer?

10 .... band does he play in?

4 Add question tags to the following statements.

1 You like pizza, ...*don't you*...... ?

2 Please come with me, ... ?

3 He didn't call, ... ?

4 Elisha lives near you, ... ?

5 Let's go to the park, ... ?

6 You had fun last night, ... ?

7 They've already sent the invitations, ... ?

5 Add questions and short answers as in the example:

1 A: Mr and Mrs Clark live in London, ...*don't they*.....?

   B: Yes, ..*they do*............. .

2 A: You visited them last summer, ... ?

   B: Yes, ...

3 A: You didn't meet their son Tony, ... ?

   B: No, ... He was in the Netherlands.

4 A: He'll be back in July, ... ?

   B: No, ... He'll still be the Netherlands.

5 A: He has been there a long time, ... ?

   B: Yes, ...

6 A: He isn't thinking of staying there, ... ?

   B: Yes, ... He likes the Netherlands a lot.

7 A: Mrs Clark will never agree to that, ... ?

   B: No, ...

6 Ask questions to which the words in bold are the answers.

Keith is a happy **11-year-old boy** who lives **in Canada**. He likes **going outside and climbing trees**. Most of all, Keith likes playing **in his tree house**. When he was 9 years old **his father** helped him build it. He just loves it! **At weekends** all of his friends come over to play in it. They have lots of fun pretending to be great explorers. When Keith grows up, he wants to be a **park ranger**. **He wants to protect the forests and the people who visit them.**

1 ... How old is Keith? ....   5 ....
2 ....   6 ....
3 ....   7 ....
4 ....   8 ....

7 🎧 |25| Listen to a telephone conversation. A boy wants to speak to William but he's not at home. For questions 1–5, complete the message to William. You will hear the conversation twice.

Phone message for you

To: William
From: Toby *Davis*
Tennis match: ☐1 at Jefferson ....
Date: ☐2 June ....
Meet at: Ryerson ☐3 ....
Time: ☐4 ....
Bring: extra tennis ☐5 ....

Infinitive (to + verb) – Gerund (verb + -ing)

🎧 **26** **Listen and repeat. Then act out.**

You seem *to be* upset. What's the matter? Will you please stop *crying*?

I don't know what *to do*. I've lost my dog. Do you mind *helping me to look* for him?

Have you thought of *putting* an advertisement in the newspaper? It's worth *trying*.

It's no use *doing* that. My dog's *too* young *to read*!

The full infinitive is used:
- **to express purpose.**
  He went **to buy** some bread.
- **after would love / like / prefer.**
  I'**d love to see** you tonight.
- **after adjectives** (angry, glad, happy, sorry, pleased, annoyed, etc.).
  I'm **glad to see** you here.
- **with too or enough.**
  He's **too** old **to drive.**
  She's clever **enough to understand** it.
- **after certain verbs** (advise, agree, appear, decide, expect, forget, hope, manage, offer, promise, refuse, seem, want, etc.).
  I **hope to meet** him again.
- **after question words** (where, how, what, who, which). Why **is not used** with *to* infinitive.
  I don't know **what to do.**
  but Nobody knew **why** he was angry.

The bare infinitive is used:
- **after modal verbs** (can, must, etc.).
  We **must leave** soon.
- **after let / make / hear / see + object.**
  My dad **lets me use** his computer.

The *-ing* form is used:
- **as a noun.**
  Smoking is dangerous.
- **after love, like, dislike, hate, enjoy, prefer.**
  I **love going** to the theatre.
- **after start, begin, stop, finish.**
  He **started doing** his homework at 5:00 pm.
- **after go for physical activities.**
  She **went skiing** last Sunday.
- **after certain verbs** (avoid, admit, confess to, deny, look forward to, mind, object to, prefer, regret, risk, spend, suggest, etc.).
  I **don't mind helping** you with the dishes.
- **after the expressions:** I'm busy, it's no use, it's (no) good, it's worth, what's the use of, be used to, there's no point (in).
  It's worth seeing that film.
- **after prepositions.**
  He left **without taking** his coat.
- **after hear, see to describe an incomplete action, that is to say that someone heard, saw only a part of the action.**
  I saw her **crossing** the street. (I saw her while she was crossing the street. I saw part of the action in progress.)
  But: hear, see + bare infinitive to describe a complete action that someone heard, saw from beginning to end.
  I saw her **cross** the street. (I saw the whole action from beginning to end.)

Infinitive (to + verb) — Gerund (verb + -ing)

> **Note:** • *Help* is followed by either the *to* infinitive or the bare infinitive.
> She **helped** me **(to) fix** the bicycle.
> • **Some verbs can take a full infinitive or the *-ing* form with no difference in
> meaning. These verbs are:** begin, hate, like, love, prefer, start, **etc.**
> He likes **to watch** / **watching** the birds.
> • **If the subject of the verb is the same as the subject of the infinitive, then the
> subject of the infinitive is omitted. If, however, the subject of the verb is
> different from the subject of the infinitive, then an object pronoun (me, you,
> him, etc.), a name (Helen) or a noun (the man) is placed before the infinitive.**
> **Compare:**   I want to be back by 10 o'clock.   I want **him** to be back by 10 o'clock.

1 Write what each word is followed by: *F.I.* (full infinitive), *B.I.* (bare infinitive) or *-ing*.

1	want	+	...*F.I.*....	8	avoid	+	....	15	shall	+	....
2	dislike	+	....	9	see	+	....	16	can	+	....
3	would love	+	....	10	promise	+	....	17	start	+	....
4	it's worth	+	....	11	expect	+	....	18	deny	+	....
5	finish	+	....	12	it's no use	+	....	19	hate	+	....
6	will	+	....	13	hope	+	....	20	must	+	....
7	make	+	....	14	let	+	....				

2 Underline the correct item.

1 Penny loves <u>**visiting**</u> / **visit** museums.

2 Jane isn't used to **get up** / **getting up** early in the morning.

3 Nikos agreed **buy** / **to buy** my old laptop.

4 **Swimming** / **To swim** keeps you fit.

5 They decided **selling** / **to sell** their old car.

6 I'm busy **to do** / **doing** my homework at the moment.

7 His teacher made him **apologise** / **to apologise** for his bad behaviour.

8 The boys went **hiking** / **to hike** in the woods yesterday.

9 His parents let him **to go** / **go** to the party.

10 Joan spent all day **to shop** / **shopping**.

11 I'd love **to visit** / **visiting** India one day.

3 Fill in the gaps with a verb from the list below. Put it in the correct form.

post	~~finish~~	lend	need	take	borrow

1 They managed ....*to finish*...... the project on time.

2 Linda may .... some help with the ironing.

3 Could you .... this parcel for me, please?

4 Dad promised .... us to the circus on Sunday.

5 Bruno won't let me .... his car.

6 She refused .... him some money.

11 Infinitive (to + verb) — Gerund (verb + -ing)

4 Rephrase the following sentences as in the example:

1 He mustn't be late for school.
I don't want ..*him to be late for*.....
.*school*.........................

2 Jim's secretary is going to attend the meeting. Jim asked her to do it.
Jim wants ....
....

3 I don't think the children should watch the late night film.
I don't want ....
....

4 Why don't you come to the concert with me?
I want ....

5 Put the verbs in brackets into the correct form.

Dear Julie,

   I am writing 1) ...*to thank*... (thank) you for the lovely birthday present. I was so happy 2) .... (receive) it. It was really nice of you to send something. On my birthday, I went with some friends to the Mexican restaurant in Poplar Street. If you haven't been, you really should 3) .... (try) it. After that, we went 4) .... (dance). It was lots of fun.

   My parents have agreed 5) .... (pay) for tennis lessons. They're glad 6) .... (see) that I'm so interested in a sport. I'm looking forward to 7) .... (have) to my first lesson this Saturday. I can't wait 8) .... (tell) you all about it.

   Well, I must 9) .... (go) now. I hope 10) .... (hear) from you soon.

Take care,

Madeleine

6 Match column A with column B to make correct sentences as in the example:

1	d	I can't stand
2		She likes
3		Thank you for
4		Do you go
5		She's looking forward
6		Windsurfing
7	'	Yes, I admit
8		It's no use

a is my favourite sport.

b to going on holiday.

c arguing with Steve. He won't change his mind.

d hearing her cry.

e painting in her free time.

f helping me with my Science project.

g cycling often?

h breaking the window.

7 Write sentences about yourself using the *infinitive* or the *-ing* form.

1 I forgot .... *to post the letter* ....
2 I enjoy ....
3 I know how ....
4 I'm busy ....
5 I can ....

6 I'm too young ....
7 I look forward to ....
8 I want ....
9 I'm happy ....
10 I've decided ....

8 In pairs, ask and answer as in the example:

1 What / you like / do / in your free time?
   A: *What do you like doing in your free time?*
   B: *I like surfing the Net.*
2 What games / you enjoy / play?

3 What kind of music / you like / listen to?
4 What films / you prefer / watch?
5 How often / you go / shop?

9 Put the verbs in brackets into the *infinitive* or the *-ing* form.

1 A: Maria, what do you like .... *doing* .... **(do)** in your free time?
   B: I love .. *listening* .. **(listen)** to music.

2 A: Do you have any plans for the summer?
   B: Yes, we've decided .... **(go)** to Madrid for our holidays.

3 A: Mum, please don't make me .... **(take)** the medicine.
   B: I know it tastes awful, Jake, but it will help you .... **(get)** better.

4 A: What's wrong with Mark?
   B: I'm not sure. He left without .... **(say)** a word.

5 A: I can't decide what .... **(wear)** to the party.
   B: Why don't you put on your red dress? It looks great on you.

6 A: Where's Daniela?
   B: She went .... **(visit)** her friend Lucy.

7 A: It's getting late. I really must .... **(go)**.
   B: All right. See you tomorrow.

8 A: I don't know how .... **(send)** a text message.
   B: I can .... **(show)** you.

9 A: Is Miss Jones in the class?
   B: Yes, I just heard her .... **(talk)** to someone.

10 A: Do you have any plans for the weekend?
   B: Alex suggested .... **(go)** camping.

11 Infinitive (to + verb) — Gerund (verb + -ing)

10 Choose the best word (A, B or C) for each space.

Yesterday, I went shopping with my sister. I wanted to 1) ..C.. her something for her birthday. She didn't really know 2) ..... to get but she seemed to like the idea of a pet, 3) ..... we went to the pet shop. She started 4) ..... at all the animals 5) ..... when she saw the puppies playing in a box, she said that she would 6) ..... to have one of them. I hoped my parents wouldn't object 7) ..... having a dog in the house. My sister promised to look after 8) ..... properly, so we bought a little brown puppy. Tomorrow, we're going to take Splash to the beach.

1	A	buys	B	buying	C	buy
2	A	why	B	what	C	where
3	A	so	B	since	C	because
4	A	looking	B	looked	C	look
5	A	even	B	still	C	but
6	A	liked	B	like	C	liking
7	A	of	B	to	C	from
8	A	them	B	they	C	it

11 Put the verbs in brackets into the correct *infinitive* or *-ing* form.

1 A: You must ...*be*... (be) worried about the race.

B: Not really. I've been training hard so I expect ...*to win*... (win).

2 A: Kate is good at .... (play) the guitar, isn't she?

B: Yes. I heard her .... (play) in a concert last week. She was great!

3 A: Mike! Could you .... (let) the dog out?

B: No. Sorry, Mum! I'm busy .... (help) Dad at the moment.

4 A: There's no point in .... (try) to do these exercises. They're too difficult.

B: You shouldn't .... (give up) so easily. Here, let me help you.

5 A: How about .... (go) to the park?

B: I'd prefer .... (stay) in and .... (watch) a DVD.

6 A: Where's Velma? I need .... (ask) her something.

B: She isn't here. She always goes .... (swim) at this time of the day.

7 A: What would you like me .... (make) for dinner?

B: Please, don't trouble yourself. Let's .... (have) a takeaway tonight — my treat!

8 A: Did Sue manage .... (get) here early today?

B: Yes, I saw her .... (work) on her computer as I came in.

12 **Fill in the gaps. Then answer the questions about yourself as in the example:**

1 What sports do you enjoy .... *playing* .... **(play)**?
   I enjoy playing tennis and golf. ....

2 Which countries would you like .... **(visit)**?
   ....

3 Name one thing that you have decided .... **(do)** next year.
   ....

4 What are you looking forward .... **(do)** next weekend?
   ....

5 How often do you go .... **(swim)** in the summer?
   ....

13 **Put the verbs in brackets into the *infinitive* or the *-ing* form.**

Tania has always loved 1) ... *dancing / to dance* .. **(dance)**. She
started 2) .... **(take)** ballet lessons when she was six
years old. She wants 3) .... **(become)** a professional
ballet dancer. She hopes 4) .... **(be)** famous one
day. In the meantime, she's looking forward to 5) ....
(take part) in the International Ballet Competition.

14 **Write sentences about you and people you know. Use the verbs in the box.**

stay	work	finish	watch	travel	get up

1 One day I'd like ....

2 My brother is looking forward to ....

3 My parents don't let ....

4 I enjoy ....

5 My best friend can't stand ....

6 My teacher doesn't mind ....

11   Infinitive (to + verb) — Gerund (verb + -ing)

Think Quick!

In teams, use the words in the list to make up sentences.

prefer	expect	can	refuse	forget	it's worth
can't stand	agree	I'm busy	want	suggest	hope
would like	look forward to	deny	enjoy	let	it's no use

Team A S1: I prefer travelling by plane.
Team B S1: I can't stand ..., etc.

Speaking Activity

(Likes / Dislikes)

Use the phrases below to find out what your partner likes/doesn't like doing in his/her free time. Use the verbs in the list.

like	love	enjoy	prefer	don't like

play games	go to the cinema	listen to music	read books	meet friends	watch TV	surf the Net

A: Do you like playing games in your free time?
B: Yes, I do. I enjoy playing chess and Monopoly, etc.

Writing Activity

Write a short paragraph about what your partner likes/doesn't like doing in his/her free time. Use the answers from the Speaking Activity.

My friend, ..., likes playing games in his/her free time. He/She
enjoys playing chess and Monopoly. He/She ....

....

....

....

....

The Passive

 27 **Listen and repeat. Then act out.**

Look at all the dust in here! It looks as if this room hasn't been cleaned for a month!

Well, don't blame me! I was only hired a week ago.

The Passive is formed with the appropriate tense of the verb to be + past participle.

	Active Voice	**Passive Voice**
Present Simple	He **delivers** letters.	Letters **are delivered**.
Past Simple	He **delivered** the letters.	The letters **were delivered**.
Present Perfect	He **has delivered** the letters.	The letters **have been delivered**.
Past Perfect	He **had delivered** the letters.	The letters **had been delivered**.
Present Continuous	He **is delivering** the letters.	The letters **are being delivered**.
Past Continuous	He **was delivering** the letters.	The letters **were being delivered**.
Future Simple	He **will deliver** the letters.	The letters **will be delivered**.
Infinitive	He has **to deliver** the letters.	The letters have **to be delivered**.
Modal + be + past part.	He **must deliver** the letters.	The letters **must be delivered**.

The Passive is used:

1 **when the agent (= the person who does the action) is unknown, unimportant or obvious from the context.**
My car **was stolen**. (We don't know who stole it.)
This church **was built** in 1815. (unimportant agent)
He **has been arrested**. (obviously by the police)

2 **to make more polite or formal statements.**
The car **hasn't been cleaned**. (more polite)
(You haven't cleaned the car. – less polite)

3 **when the action is more important than the agent, as in processes, instructions, events, reports, headlines, news items, and advertisements.**
30 people **were killed** in the earthquake.

4 **to put emphasis on the agent.**
The new library will be opened **by the Queen**.

12 ## The Passive

Changing from Active into Passive

- The object of the active verb becomes the subject in the new sentence.

	Subject	Verb	Object	(agent)
Active	Picasso	painted	that picture.	
Passive	That picture	**was painted**		by Picasso.

- The active verb changes into a passive form and the subject of the active verb becomes the agent. The agent is introduced with **by** or it is omitted.
  After modal verbs (will, can, must, have to, should, may, ought to) we use be + past participle.
  You **can** use the machine for cutting bread. ⇨ The machine **can be used** for cutting bread.
- We use **by + agent** to say who or what carries out the action. We use **with + instrument / material / ingredient** to say what the agent used.
  A cake was made **by Tina.** It was made **with eggs, flour and sugar.**
- We put the agent (= the person who does the action) into the passive sentence only if it adds information. When the agent is unknown, unimportant or obvious it is omitted. Agents such as people (in general), they, somebody, etc. are omitted.
  Alexander Graham Bell invented the telephone.
  The telephone was invented **by Alexander Graham Bell**. (The agent is not omitted because it adds information.)
  Somebody pushed him. He was pushed (by somebody). (Unknown agent is omitted.)
  The police arrested him. He was arrested (by the police). (Obvious agent is omitted.)

1 Fill in: *is*, *are*, *was* or *were*.

1 A short story competition ......*is*..... organised by our school every year.
2 The electric light bulb ....*was*.... invented by Thomas Edison in 1879.
3 Many films ..*are*.. produced in Hollywood.
4 The Lost City of the Incas .....*is*.... located in Peru.
5 The film *Titanic* ..*was*.... directed by James Cameron.
6 The Special Olympics World Games ....*were*..... held every four years.
7 *Guernica* ...*was*.... painted by Pablo Picasso.
8 Toyota cars ...*are*... made in Japan.

9 Penicillin ..*was*.... discovered by Alexander Fleming.
10 The Harry Potter books ......*were*.... written by J. K. Rowling.
11 The music for the *Phantom of the Opera* ....*is*.... composed by Andrew Lloyd Webber.
12 The Parthenon ......*were*...... visited by thousands of tourists each year.
13 Breakfast ......*is*..... served from 7:00 am to 11:00 am daily.
14 The Coliseum ....*are*..... completed by the Romans in 80 AD.
15 Coffee ...*was*.. grown in Brazil.

2 How are music videos made? Turn the following
sentences into the *present simple passive*.

1 The music producer chooses the song for the music video.
The song for the music video is chosen by the music producer.

2 A director directs the music video.
The music video is directed by a director

3 A cameraman shoots the video.
The video shots by a cameraman

4 A singer or band sings the song.
The song sung by a singer or band.

5 The music company produces the music video.
The music vt deoproduced by the music company

---

3 Put the verbs in brackets into the *past simple passive*.

Two men 1) *were seen* (see) breaking into a house last night. The police
2) *was called* (call) and one man 3) *was caught* (catch) immediately. The other
escaped but he 4) *was found* (find) soon after. Both men 5) *were taken* (take)
to the police station where they 6) *were questioned* (question) separately by a police officer. The
two men 7) *were charged* (charge) with burglary.

---

4 Amy and many other volunteers are helping their town get ready for the
Carnival. Put the verbs in brackets into the *present continuous
passive* and the *past continuous passive.*

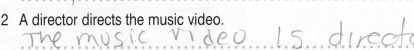

A It's 10 o'clock on Friday morning and the volunteers are busy.

1 At this time, coloured lights *are being put up* (put up).
2 Colourful ribbons *are being tied around trees* (tie) around trees.
3 The music *is being chosen* (choose).
4 The costumes *are being checked* (check).
5 A stage *is being built* (build) in the square.

B Later that day, Amy arrived to help with the preparations.

1 When she got there, the streets *were being decorated* (decorate).
2 Food and drinks *were delivered* (deliver).
3 Tables and chairs *were being placed* (place) in the square.
4 Popcorn *were being made* (make).

12 The Passive

5 Fill in the correct *passive* form.

Mr Pryce was having some home improvements done. Write what he saw when he went to inspect the work.

1 The windows ..*had been cleaned*... **(clean)**
2 New curtains ..had been put up.. **(put up)**
3 The walls ...had been painted... **(paint)**
4 Light fittings ..had been installed.. **(install)**
5 Some furniture ..had been delivered.. **(deliver)**
6 New carpets ..had been bought... **(buy)**

6 Turn from *active* into *passive*. Omit the agent where it can be omitted.

1 Someone has broken the crystal vase.
The crystal vase has been broken.
(omitted)

2 His parents have brought him up to be polite.
He has been brought up to be polite.

3 Alexander Bain invented the fax machine.
The fax machine was invented by Alexander Bain

4 A famous designer will redecorate the hotel.
The hotel will be redecorate by a famous designer.

5 They will advertise the product on TV.
The product on TV will be advertise

6 The gardener has planted some trees.
Some trees has been planted by the gardener

7 Put the verbs in brackets into the correct *passive* tense.

1 A: Those shoes look so comfortable.
   B: They ..*were made*.. **(make)** in Italy.

2 A: Why didn't you fly to Moscow?
   B: Because all the flights were cancelled **(cancel)** due to a snowstorm.
   When was lunch served
   'lunch/serve)?
   om 11:30 am to 2:30 pm.

4 A: Who invented the first computer game
   (the first computer game/invent/by)?
   B: Steve Russell.

5 A: Can I bring my dog?
   B: I'm afraid pets are not allowed **(not/allow)** in the camp.

6 A: Why didn't you come to Helen's party?
   B: I was not invited **(not/invite)**.

> When we want to find out who or what did something the passive question form
> is as follows: Who / What ... by?
> **Who** was the TV invented by? **What** was the fire caused by?

8 Using the *passive*, ask questions to which the bold type words are the
answers.

1 **Captain Cook** discovered Australia. *Who was Australia discovered by ?*
2 We keep money **in a safe**. *Who keeps the money safe ?*
3 **A bee** stung him. *What stung him ?*
4 They speak **English** in New Zealand. *What do they speak in New Zealand*
5 They have taken **his aunt** to hospital. *who has taken his aunt to the hospital ?*
6 **The boys** damaged the TV. *Who damaged the TV ?*
7 **Da Vinci** painted the *Mona Lisa*. *Who painted the Mona Visa ?*
8 He invited **30 people** to his party. *Who invited 30 people to the party ?*
9 They grow bananas **in Africa**. *Who grown the bananas in Africa ?* *grows*
10 Versace designed **these glasses**. *Who designed these glasses ?*

9 Fill in *by* or *with*.

1 The photos were taken ...*with*... a
   digital camera.
2 *The Green Mile* was written ...*by*...
   Stephen King.
3 The sauce was made ...*with*...
   onions and peppers.
4 The room was decorated ...*with*...
   flowers.
5 *Amelia* was directed ...*by*... Mira
   Nair.
6 The treasure chest was opened ...*with*...
   a special key.

10 Turn from *active* into *passive*.

1 You must leave the bathroom tidy. *The bathroom must be left tidy.*
2 You should water this plant daily. *The plant should be watered daily*
3 Our neighbour ought to paint the garage. *The garage ought to be paint*
4 I have to return these books to the library. *The books have to be returned to the library*
5 They must pay their phone bill. *The phone bill must be payed*
6 You should lock the front door. *The front door should be locked*
7 You must sign these papers. *These papers must be signed*
8 He has to deliver the parcel. *The parcel has to be delivered*
9 You ought to put your toys away. *The toys ought to be put away*
10 We must protect the environment. *The environment must be protected.*

12 The Passive

> With verbs taking two objects it is more usual to begin the passive sentence with the person.
>
> I sent **her** some roses. **She** was sent some roses. (more usual) or
> **Some roses** were sent to her. (less usual)

11 Turn from *active* into *passive* as in the example:

1 He gave me a present.
   I was given a present.
   A present was given to me.

2 The waiter will bring us the bill.

3 The Queen presented him with a medal.

4 Amy showed me some photos.

5 Jill sent Juan a letter.

6 Her mother bought Olga some sweets.

7 Bob has sold Ted a second-hand car.

8 Larry is going to send a letter to Tom.

12 Rewrite the newspaper headlines as complete sentences.

① FOOTBALLER OFFERED MILLION POUNDS FOR TRANSFER

② 3-YEAR-OLD TAKEN TO HOSPITAL AFTER SERIOUS FALL YESTERDAY

③ MONEY BEING RAISED FOR BABY'S OPERATION IN USA

④ PLANET BEING DESTROYED BY POLLUTION

⑤ TREASURE DISCOVERED IN OLD LADY'S GARDEN

⑥ NO CAMERAS ALLOWED IN MUSEUM

⑦ ANIMALS BEING USED TO TEST BEAUTY PRODUCTS

⑧ RARE PICASSO PAINTING TO BE EXHIBITED AT NATIONAL GALLERY NEXT MONDAY

⑨ TOM CRUISE ASKED TO SPONSOR CHARITY EVENT YESTERDAY

1 ..... *The footballer has been offered a million pounds for the transfer.* .....

2

3

4

5

6

7

8

9

13 **Rewrite the following passage in the *passive*.**

Our school is organising a Science Fair. The headmaster will choose the best project. The teachers have asked students to do something about the environment. Students should include interesting experiments in their projects. The school will give the winners a set of Science books.

A Science Fair is being organised by the teachers of our school.

....

....

....

....

....

14 **A reporter is talking to Lucy Fame. Complete the interview.**

Rep: It's wonderful to interview such a famous person as you.

Lucy: Yes, you are very lucky!

Rep: I know that you 1) .... *have been interviewed* .... **(interview)** many times before.

Lucy: Yes, I have.

Rep: Also, I know that three books 2) ....
.... **(already/write)** about you.

Lucy: Yes, they have – and another one 3) .... **(write)** at the moment.

Rep: A film 4) .... **(make)** about your life two years ago, wasn't it?

Lucy: Yes, it was a brilliant film! The leading role 5) .... **(play)** by a beautiful young actress.

Rep: 6) .... any more films .... **(make)** in the future?

Lucy: Oh yes, of course!

Rep: Where do you buy your clothes from, Lucy?

Lucy: I don't buy them! They 7) .... **(design)** especially for me.

Rep: And what about your fabulous house?

Lucy: It 8) .... **(build)** five years ago by an Italian architect.

Rep: You must make a lot of money.

Lucy: I make lots of money and everybody loves me. Flowers 9) ....
(send) to my house every day.

Rep: Not by me, that's for certain!

12   The Passive

(Talking about monuments)

In pairs use the information and the notes below to ask and answer questions as in the example:

- where / located
- what / made of
- when / completed
- who / designed by
- why / built

Name:	the Taj Mahal
Located:	in Agra, in the northern state of Uttar Pradesh, in India
Made of:	white marble
Designed by:	Ustad Ahmad Lahani
Completed:	in 1653
Reason built:	in memory of Emperor Shah Jahan's favourite wife, Mumtaz Mahal

A: Where is the Taj Mahal located?

B: It is located in Agra, in the northern state of Uttar Pradesh, in India, etc.

Writing Activity

Use the information about the Taj Mahal from the Speaking Activity and write a short paragraph about it.

The Taj Mahal is located in Agra, in the northern state of Uttar Pradesh, in India. It . . . .

. . . .

. . . .

. . . .

. . . .

. . . .

. . . .

1 **Put the verbs in brackets into the correct *infinitive* form.**

1 I expect . . . . **(be)** back
   by dinnertime.
2 Will you help me . . . .
   (carry) these bags?
3 Please, let me . . . .
   (borrow) your textbook.
4 The committee agreed . . . .
   (hear) us out.

5 We'll be glad . . . .
   (send) you all the information.
6 The teacher made me . . . .
   (stay) after school.
7 Don't they want . . . . **(join)**
   us for tea?
8 You must . . . . **(wait)**
   your turn.

2 **Fill in the gaps using the *infinitive* or *-ing* form.**

1 A: Do you fancy . . . .
   . . . . **(go)** out tonight?
   B: Not really. I'm tired of . . . .
   . . . . **(eat)** out.

2 A: Did you go to the dentist's today?
   B: Yes. She advised me . . . .
   . . . . **(brush)** my teeth regularly.

3 A: Why are you so angry?
   B: I can't stand . . . .
   . . . . **(wait)** in the queue any longer.

4 A: Did you remember . . . .
   . . . . **(walk)** the dog?
   B: Yes, but I forgot . . . .
   . . . . **(lock)** the gate.

5 A: Should I apply for the cashier's post?
   B: It's definitely worth . . . .
   . . . . **(try)** for it.

6 A: You told Sarah, didn't you?
   B: Of course not! I promised not . . . .
   . . . . **(say)** anything.

3 **Put the verbs in brackets into the correct form.**

Last Sunday, I decided 1) ....*to explore*.... **(explore)** the old house near our village. My little brother refused 2) . . . . **(come)** because he was frightened but my friend Jeff said he didn't mind 3) . . . . **(go)** with me. We arrived at the house late one evening and began 4) . . . . **(climb)** the old wooden stairs. When we reached the top it was so dark that I couldn't see anything. To my horror, Jeff seemed to have disappeared. Suddenly, I heard something 5) . . . . **(make)** a strange noise which made my hair 6) . . . . **(stand)** on end. At first, I thought it was Jeff who was pretending 7) . . . . **(be)** a ghost. Then Jeff appeared behind me. We were scared. We didn't know what 8) . . . . **(do)**. We thought we'd better 9) . . . . **(leave)** the house quickly. When I told my parents what had happened they made me 10) . . . . **(promise)** not 11) . . . . **(go)** there again.

Progress Check 6

4 Put the verbs in brackets into the correct *passive* tense.

1 A: Are you coming to Tom's party?
   B: Unfortunately, *I haven't been invited* (not/invite).

2 A: Where can I find interesting facts for my project on dinosaurs?
   B: All the information you need .... (can/find) at the library.

3 A: Who .... (Mona Lisa/paint)?
   B: Leonardo da Vinci, of course!

4 A: Do you know when the Grammy Awards are?
   B: Yes, they .... (hold) every year in February.

5 A: A new library .... (build) in our town at the moment.
   B: Yes, I know. It .... (open) by the mayor when it's finished.

5 Turn from *active* into *passive*. Omit the agent where it can be omitted.

1 Someone has stolen my wallet. *My wallet has been stolen.*

2 Jon Favreau directed *Iron Man*. ....

3 The doctor has examined him. ....

4 They will make the announcement tomorrow.

5 Emma designed this dress. ....

6 People make jam from fruit. ....

7 Jason broke the window. ....

8 A burglar broke into our house last night. ...

9 Marie Curie discovered radium. ....

10 They serve breakfast every morning at 7:00. ....

6 Turn from *active* into *passive*.

1 They are promoting her. .... *She is being promoted.* ....
2 A famous architect designed these buildings. ....
3 Van Gogh painted that picture. ....
4 You must complete this work today. ....
5 The Queen will open the exhibition. ....
6 Lightning has struck the tree. ....

122

7 **Turn the following passage into the *passive*.**

Someone found a skeleton in a cave in the mountains yesterday. They have sent it to a laboratory. Scientists were examining it all through the night. They have discovered that it is the skeleton of a dinosaur from thousands of years ago. They are still doing tests. They are going to send it to a museum when they have completed the tests.

A skeleton was found in a cave in the mountains yesterday. ....

....

....

....

....

Listening

8 **🎧 28** **You will hear some information about an art gallery. Listen and complete questions 1-5. You will hear the information twice.**

Greenwood Art Gallery

Thomas Moore built it in: *1884*

Number of paintings: **1** ....

A few paintings are by: **2** Margaret ....

She painted pictures of: **3** large ....

Sculptures: **4** of clay, rock and ....

Closing time: **5** ....

13

🎧 **29** **Listen and repeat. Then act out.**

Type 0	*if*-clause (hypothesis)	Main clause (result)	Use
general truth	if / when + Present Simple	Present Simple	something which is always true, laws of nature

If you **heat** ice, it **melts**.

Type 1	*if*-clause (hypothesis)	Main clause (result)	Use
real present	if + Present Simple unless (= if not)	Future, Imperative can / must / may + bare infinitive	real or very probable situation in the present or future

If he **comes** late, we**'ll miss** the bus.

If you **can't afford** it, **don't buy** it. = Unless you **can** afford it, **don't buy** it.

If you **see** her, **can you give** her a message?

Type 2	*if*-clause (hypothesis)	Main clause (result)	Use
unreal present	if + Past Simple	would / could / might + bare infinitive	improbable situation in the present or future; also used to give advice

If I **were** you, I **would see** a doctor. (advice)

If I **had** money, I **could buy** a new car. (But I don't have enough money to buy one.) (improbable situation)

Type 3	*if*-clause (hypothesis)	Main clause (result)	Use
unreal past	if + Past Perfect	would / could / might + have + past participle	unreal or improbable situation in the past; also used to express regret and criticism

If you **hadn't been** rude, he **wouldn't have punished** you. (But you were rude and he punished you.) (criticism)

Study the following notes:

- **We put a comma after the *if*-clause when it comes first.**
  If we go by plane, it will be more expensive.
  It will be more expensive if we go by plane.

- **Unless means if not.**
  We'll go for a picnic **unless** it rains.
  We'll go for a picnic **if** it does**n't** rain.

- **After if, we can use were instead of was in all persons.**
  If I **were** you, I wouldn't spend so much money.

- **We do not usually use will, would or should in an *if*-clause.**
  If **we take** a taxi, we won't be late.
  NOT If we will take a taxi, we won't be late.
  However, we use should after if when we are not sure about a possibility.
  If I see him, I'll give it to him. (Perhaps I will see him.)
  If I **should** see him, I'll give it to him. (Perhaps I'll see him but I'm not sure.)

1 **Match the following parts of the sentences.**

1 If it's sunny tomorrow,   A we'll make a snowman.   1 ...*D*....
2 If John doesn't hurry,   B she'll have to take a taxi.   2 ....
3 If it snows,   C he'll be late.   3 ....
4 If there are no buses,   D we'll go on a picnic.   4 ....

2 **Write *type 1 conditionals*.**

1 (eat/put on weight)
If he eats so much, he will put on weight.

2 (not work hard/lose job)

3 (rain/stay at home)

3 **Put the verbs in brackets into the correct tense. Add a comma where necessary.**

1 If the dog .... *keeps* .... **(keep)** barking, the neighbours will complain.

2 The teacher .... **(be)** angry if you come late for school again.

3 If I .... **(finish)** my homework early I'll go out with my friends.

4 If the weather is bad on Saturday we .....
.... **(stay)** at home.

5 You should see a doctor if you ....
.... **(not/feel)** well.

6 If you study hard you ....
.... **(pass)** your exam.

⑬ Conditionals

④ Fill in: *unless* or *if*.

1 .... *If* .... you make so much noise, I won't be able to sleep.

2 You won't understand .... you listen carefully.

3 I won't be able to finish the work .... you help me.

4 .... you're hungry, I'll make you a sandwich.

5 We'll miss the bus .... we hurry.

6 They won't be able to buy a house .... they save money.

7 I'll tell you .... you get any messages.

8 I'll come with you to the dentist's .... you want to go alone.

⑤ Match the items in column A with those in column B in order to make correct *type 0 conditional* sentences as in the example:

..1-e .... *If / When you drop a stone in water, the stone sinks.* ....

A	B
1 Drop a stone in water.	a The water boils.
2 Pour oil on water.	b The ball falls to the ground.
3 Heat water to 100°C.	c The chocolate melts.
4 Mix blue and yellow.	d The food stays fresh longer.
5 Throw a ball into the air.	e The stone sinks.
6 Heat chocolate.	f The water becomes ice.
7 Freeze water.	g You get green.
8 Put food in the fridge.	h It floats.

⑥ Put the verbs in brackets into the correct tense.

1 A: I must be at the airport by 9:00 am.
   B: Well, if you *don't leave* (not/leave) right away, you ..... *will miss* ...... (miss) your flight.

2 A: How long will you stay in Europe?
   B: I .... (not/stay) long unless I .... (find) a summer job.

3 A: I need some help with the housework.
   B: Well, if you .... (hoover) the carpets, I .... (make) the beds.

4 A: How can I print this information?
   B: I .... (show) you if you .... (wait) a few minutes.

7 **Put the verbs in brackets into the correct tense.**

Pat is feeling unhappy. If she 1) ...*joined*.... **(join)** an after school club, she
2) .... **(make)** more friends. Pat 3) .... **(enjoy)**
herself if she 4) .... **(go)** out more. Her school marks are suffering,
too. If she 5) .... **(study)** more, she 6) ....
(have) better marks and she 7) .... **(get)** into university.
Also, she doesn't exercise much. She 8) .... **(feel)**
healthier if she 9) .... **(walk)** to school and she
10) .... **(have)** more energy if she
11) .... **(add)** vegetables to her diet.

8 **What would you do in each situation? Write *type 2 conditionals*.**

call an ambulance	run away	try to catch it
~~complain to the manager~~	ring the police	walk to the nearest garage

1 You find a fly in your
   soup.

If I found a fly in my
soup, I would complain
to the manager.

2 You see a burglar
   breaking into your house.

3 You see a mouse in your
   kitchen.

4 Your car runs out of
   petrol.

5 You see an accident.

6 You see a ghost in your
   room.

13   Conditionals

9   **Advise Mei what to do in each situation.**

- get / haircut
- ~~clean / glasses~~
- go / dentist
- buy / burger
- take / break
- put on / jumper

1   M: I can't see a thing.
    Y: *If I were you, I'd clean my glasses!*

2   M: I'm tired.
    Y: ....

3   M: I'm hungry.
    Y: ....

4   M: I'm really cold.
    Y: ....

5   M: My hair's a mess.
    Y: ....

6   M: I've got a toothache.
    Y: ....

10   **Match the parts of the sentences.**

1 If I hadn't missed the bus,	A he would have gone to university.	1 ...G...
2 If she hadn't felt ill this morning,	B the dog wouldn't have got out.	2 ....
3 If the food hadn't been awful,	C Chris wouldn't have given me flowers.	3 ....
4 If he had passed his exams,	D she would have gone to school.	4 ....
5 If the salary had been good,	E I would have accepted the job.	5 ....
6 If it hadn't been my birthday,	F he would have been able to buy a car.	6 ....
7 If Ben had saved some money,	G I wouldn't have been late for work.	7 ....
8 If Katia had closed the gate,	H we would have eaten it.	8 ....

128

11 **Write *type 3 conditionals* as in the example:**

1   (ladder/break/not hurt his leg)

If the ladder hadn't broken, he wouldn't have hurt his leg.

2   (drive carefully/not have accident)

....
....
....
....

3   (John run faster/win race)

....
....
....
....

12 **Read the story and write *type 3 conditional* sentences as in the example:**

Last night there was a terrible storm and there was a power cut. In the morning Greg's alarm clock didn't ring, so he woke up late. Sadly, he missed the bus and wasn't on time for an important meeting with a new client. His boss was upset with him.

1   *If there hadn't been a terrible storm, there wouldn't have been a power cut.*

2   *If there hadn't been a power cut,* ....

3   ....

4   ....

5   ....

6   ....

13 Conditionals

13 Write *type 0, 1, 2 or 3 conditionals*. Then write the types of conditionals.

1 (you not study/not pass exams)

If you don't study, you won't pass the exams. (1st type, real present)

2 (he have money/he buy a burger)

3 (you not put on coat/you catch a cold)

4 (she not fall over/not break the plates)

5 (he not play with matches/ he burn his finger)

6 (you drop ice in water/it float)

14 Put the verbs in brackets into the correct tense.

1 A: Do you know where the nearest bank is?
   B: Yes, if you ....*turn*.... **(turn)** left at the traffic lights, you ....*'ll see*...... **(see)** one on your right.

2 A: I don't know what to do about my problem.
   B: If I .... **(be)** you, I .... **(talk)** to my parents.

3 A: Where .... **(you/go)** if you ....**(have)** a week off?
   B: Well, probably to New York.

4 A: If you .... **(go)** to the supermarket, ... **(you/buy)** some lemons and carrots for me?
   B: Of course.

5 A: Dad, I failed the Maths test.
   B: If you .... **(study)** harder, you .... **(not/fail)** it.

6 A: Can I go to the park, Mum?
   B: No, not unless you .... **(finish)** your homework.

15 Use Thomas' thoughts to write conditionals as in the example. Then write the types of conditionals.

THOMAS IS ON A DESERT ISLAND.

1 I'll make a hut. I don't want to sleep under the trees.

2 I don't have a bottle. I can't send a message.

3 I didn't save the radio transmitter. I can't call for help.

4 There are too many sharks and I can't escape.

5 I'm by myself. I feel lonely.

6 I'll find some coconuts. Then I will be able to drink some coconut milk.

7 I haven't got a knife. I can't cut any branches down.

8 I hope someone will find me, or else I'll never see my family again.

1 If I make a hut, I won't have to sleep under the trees. (1st type, real present)
2 ....
3 ....
4 ....
5 ....
6 ....
7 ....
8 ....

16 Complete the sentences about yourself with the correct conditional.

1 If I had a garden, ...

2 If it's rainy tomorrow, ...

3 If I had tried harder, ...

4 I might have gone out with my friends . . . .
   . . . .

5 Unless I have time, ...

6 I would ask for my friends' help . . . .
   . . . .

7 I may go to the cinema . . . .

8 I could be fitter . . . .

9 If I had been more careful, ...

10 If I saw someone in danger, ...

Chain Story

Tony has gone to a restaurant with some friends. In teams, make type 1 conditionals about Tony using the phrases in the list.

- get home late • go bed late • not wake up early • miss bus
- his boss get angry • not give holiday • not be able visit family

Teacher: If he gets home late, he'll go to bed late.
Team A S1: If he goes to bed late, he ..., etc.

Speaking Activity

(Giving advice)

Work in pairs. What advice can you give your friend who wants to lose weight?

| stop eating sweets | eat fruit - vegetables | go to gym | start swimming | walk to school |

A: If I were you, I would stop eating sweets.
B: If I were you, I would eat more fruit and vegetables, etc.

Writing Activity

Use your answers from the Speaking Activity to write a short email to your English pen friend about what to do to lose weight.

Dear Frank,

There are a lot of things you can do to lose weight.

If I were you, I would stop eating sweets. Also, ...

....

....

....

....

Take care,

Nick

30 **Listen and repeat. Then act out.**

I wish I had lived hundreds of years ago.

Why? Do you wish you had been a famous explorer like Christopher Columbus?

No, I just wish I didn't have so much history to learn.

- **I wish (if only) + Past Simple (wish about the present)**
  We express a wish about a present situation which we want to be different.
  I wish he **were/was** with us now.

- **I wish (if only) + subject + could + bare infinitive (wish about the present)**
  We use this pattern for a wish or regret in the present concerning lack of ability.
  I wish he **could** learn faster.

- **I wish (if only) + subject + would + bare infinitive (wish about the future)**
  (we never say: I wish I would)
  We express a wish for a change in the future.
  I wish they **would build a new** library.

- **I wish (if only) + Past Perfect (regret about the past)**
  We express a regret or a wish that something happened or didn't happen in the past.
  I wish he **hadn't failed** his test.

- **If only** means the same as 'I wish' but it is more emphatic.
  I wish he could help me. **If only** he could help me. (stronger, more emphatic)

- **After 'I wish' we may use 'were' instead of 'was' in all persons.**
  I wish I **was/were** rich.

14   **Wishes**

1   **Ann doesn't like her new house. Write what she wishes.**

> The house is so old and dirty. She has to paint it. The house doesn't have central heating. The kitchen is small.

1   *I wish the house wasn't/weren't so old and dirty.*

2

3

4

2   **Pedro wants things to be different in the future. Write what he wishes.**

> I want my father to give me more pocket money. I want my sister to stop using my computer. I don't want my mother to make me eat vegetables. I don't want my brother to take my skateboard.

1   *I wish my father would give me more pocket money.*

2

3

4

3   **Ted regrets what he did or didn't do. Write what he wishes.**

> Ted was naughty in class. He didn't hear the teacher's question. She got angry with him. The teacher wrote a note to his parents.

1   *I wish I hadn't been naughty in class.*

2

3

4

4   **a) Read the wishes. Which refers to the: present? future? past?**

1   If only I was famous.   *present*

2   I wish I hadn't lost the game.

3   I wish I could come with you.

4   I wish it would stop raining.

     b) Write similar sentences about yourself.

5 **Write what each person wishes. Then fill in:** *wish about the present, regret about the past, wish about the future.*

1   He broke his leg.

I wish I hadn't
broken my leg.
(regret about the
past)

2   Laura plays her music very loud.

....
....
....
....

3   It's raining.

....
....
....
....

4   He didn't go to football practice yesterday.

....
....
....

5   He crashed his dad's car last night.

....
....
....

6   She can't type fast. She won't get the job.

....
....
....

7   He talks too much and she doesn't like it.

....
....
....

8   His car is very old but he can't buy a new one.

....
....
....

9   He stayed out late last night.

....
....
....

14 Wishes

6 Tanya is a famous young singer. These are some of the things she doesn't like about being famous. Read what she says and write sentences as in the example:

- People always ask me to sing at parties.
- I have to look my best all the time.
- Sometimes magazines write false things about me.

- I don't have much time to see my friends.
- I can't go out by myself.
- Photographers follow me everywhere.

1 *I wish people wouldn't always ask me to sing at parties.*
2 ....
3 ....
4 ....
5 ....
6 ....

7 Write what these people wish they *had/hadn't done* as in the example:

1 John drove his car so fast that he had an accident.

John: *I wish I hadn't driven my car so fast. I wouldn't have had an accident.*

2 Nastasia was late and she missed the beginning of the film.

Nastasia: ....

3 Jack ate too much and he got sick.

Jack: ....

4 Mitsuko was in a hurry and she forgot her purse at home.

Mitsuko: ....

5 Susan didn't take off her ring before she went swimming and she lost it in the sea.

Susan: ....

6 Hans and Jane didn't save any money so they didn't go on holiday last summer.

Hans & Jane: ....

8 **Put the verbs in brackets into the correct tense.**

1 A: We're so late! I wish we *had taken* **(take)** the metro.

B: Next time, we'll know better.

2 A: If only I . . . . **(not/be)** so rude to Bill.

B: Why don't you apologise? I'm sure he'll forgive you.

3 A: Are you going to Kim's party on Saturday?

B: No. I wish I . . . . **(go)**. I'm sure it'll be fun.

4 A: I wish Helen . . . . **(tell)** us what's bothering her.

B: Yes. She seems really upset, doesn't she?

5 A: If only Jack . . . . **(call)** me. I'm so worried.

B: I'm sure he will as soon as he arrives in Los Angeles.

6 A: I wish I . . . . **(know)** how to use this camera.

B: Don't worry. I'll show you.

7 A: I wish I . . . . **(not/forget)** to pay the bills.

B: Never mind. You can do it tomorrow.

8 A: I wish Akim . . . . **(come)** to the concert with us.

B: So do I. He would have really enjoyed it.

9 **Write wishes using the words in bold in the sentences as in the example:**

1 **You left the radio on** and now the batteries don't work.

You say, " *I wish I hadn't left the radio on.* "

2 It's very dark outside and **you can't find your torch**.

You say, " . . . . "

3 **You didn't do your homework** and your teacher is angry.

You say, " . . . . "

4 You live in the city. **You prefer the countryside**.

You say, " . . . . "

5 It's raining outside and **you want it to stop**.

You say, " . . . . "

6 **You stayed up late last night** and today you're very tired.

You say, " . . . . "

7 You are having a party **but nobody has come yet**.

You say, " . . . . "

8 You have short, straight hair. **You would like long, curly hair**.

You say, " . . . . "

9 You have just left your house and **left your keys at home**.

You say, " . . . . "

10 It is winter and **it doesn't look like it is going to snow**.

You say, " . . . . "

14 Wishes

10 Complete the wishes and then make conditional sentences as in the example:

1

> I got wet. I should have taken my raincoat with me.

I wish *I had taken my raincoat with me.*

If *I had taken my raincoat with me, I wouldn't have got wet.*

2

> I can't buy a sports car. I don't have enough money.

I wish ....

If ....

3

> I failed my exams. I should have studied harder.

I wish ....

If ....

4

> I have too much homework to do. I can't go out with my friends.

I wish ....

If ....

Speaking Activity

(Expressing wishes / regrets)

In pairs, take turns to tell each other your wishes or regrets.

A: I wish I had a bike. If I had a bike, I could ride it to school.

B: If only / I wish I hadn't failed any exams. If I had passed my exams, I would have been able to go to university, etc.

Writing Activity

Use your partner's answers from the Speaking Activity to write a paragraph about his/her wishes / regrets.

Tony wishes he had a bike. ....

....

....

....

....

1 Put the verbs in brackets into the correct tense.

1 If I were you, I ......*would call*...... **(call)** the police.

2 If he .... **(drive)** more carefully, he wouldn't have crashed the car.

3 I won't go to the party unless you .... **(come)** with me.

4 If she hadn't left the door open, the cat ... . **(not/run away)**.

5 If you .... **(see)** Bill, can you ask him to call me?

6 If I .... **(have)** enough money, I'd buy a computer.

7 Unless you apologise, Margaret .... **(not/forgive)** you.

8 If they .... **(not/rob)** the bank, the police wouldn't have sent them to prison.

9 If it .... **(rain)**, we won't go to the park.

10 If I had known about their business plans, I .... **(tell)** you.

11 If you go to Cairo, you .... **(see)** the Pyramids.

2 Use the man's thoughts to write conditionals.

1 I didn't pay much attention. I crashed the car.

2 I was on the phone. I didn't see the tree.

3 I didn't see the tree. I crashed into it.

4 I haven't got much money. I won't be able to pay for repairs.

5 I wore my seatbealt. I didn't hurt myself.

6 I'll drive more carefully in the future. I won't have another accident.

1 .*If I had paid more attention, I wouldn't have crashed the car.*...........

2 ....

3 ....

4 ....

5 ....

6 ....

3 Finish the following sentences.

1 If I had enough money, *I'd buy a new pair of shoes.*

2 I wouldn't say that to her

3 If you don't wake up on time,

4 We'll stay at home

5 If you didn't go to the gym so often,

6 Unless you invite her to the party,

7 She wouldn't have forgotten the appointment

8 We would have reached the airport on time

9 If you drive so carelessly,

10 If I had got to the station earlier,

4 Fill in the correct form of the verbs in brackets.

1 I wish I *hadn't forgotten* (not/forget) her birthday.

2 If only I (have) the money to buy a new car.

3 Steve wishes he (speak) so rudely to his boss because he fired him.

4 If only she (tell) him the truth. He wouldn't be so angry with her.

5 Tom wishes he (not/have) so much homework to do.

6 I wish I (not/break) my sister's doll. She wouldn't be sad now.

7 I wish she (stop) interrupting me all the time.

8 Mrs Jones wishes she (speak) a foreign language.

9 If only I (be) taller. I would join the basketball team.

10 He wishes he (not/crash) his father's car. Now his father is upset.

11 I wish Mum (let) me go to the party next week.

5 Read the people's comments and write what they wish.

1 Bill: I have to tidy my room.

   I wish I didn't have to tidy my room.

2 Melek: I missed the plane to Rome.

3 Manos: I want my dad to buy me a computer.

4 Laura: I can't drive a car.

5 Mike: My room is so small.

6 **Read what Matt is saying and write what he wishes.**

I've always wanted to travel to Bali. I don't have any money. I've lost my job. I can't find another job. I don't have any friends. I feel lonely.

1 *I wish I could travel to Bali.*

2 ....

3 ....

4 ....

5 ....

6 ....

Listening 🎧

7 🎧 **31** **Listen to Samantha talking to Julie on the phone about joining a gym. For questions 1–5, tick (✓) A, B, or C. You will hear the conversation twice. Look at questions 1–5 now. You have 20 seconds.**

0 Julie joined the gym

   A one week ago. ☐

   B two weeks ago. ☐

   C last month. ✓

1 Samantha wants to join a gym because

   A she wants to lose weight. ☐

   B it is cheap for students. ☐

   C Joan is at the gym. ☐

2 To join the gym, Samantha will need

   A her passport and her student card. ☐

   B her student card and a doctor's note. ☐

   C a doctor's note and her passport. ☐

3 The cost of the gym per month is

   A € 120. ☐

   B € 10. ☐

   C € 20. ☐

4 Members need to sign up earlier to use the

   A swimming pool. ☐

   B aerobics classes. ☐

   C tennis courts. ☐

5 A personal trainer costs an extra

   A € 5. ☐

   B € 25. ☐

   C € 50. ☐

Relatives

Listen and repeat. Then act out.

Relative Pronouns (**who, whose, whom, which, that**) **introduce relative clauses.**

	subject of the verb of the relative clause (can't be omitted)	object of the verb of the relative clause (can be omitted)	possession (can't be omitted)
used for people	who / that	who / whom / that	whose
	She's the teacher **who** / **that** came to our school last week.	I saw a friend (**who** / **whom** / **that**) I hadn't seen for years.	That's the boy **whose** brother won the prize.
used for things / animals	which / that	which / that	whose / of which
	This is the house **which** / **that** belongs to my friend.	Here's the bag (**which** / **that**) you left on my desk.	That's the bag **whose** handle is broken.

- **That** replaces **who** or **which** but is never used after commas or prepositions. **That** usually follows superlatives and words like *something, nothing, anything, all, none, many, few.*
  Ann, **who** is very clever, did the puzzle in five minutes. ('**That**' can't be used here.)
  She's the **tallest** girl **that** I've ever seen.
  There's **something that** you don't know.
- **Prepositions in Relative Clauses. We avoid using prepositions before relative pronouns.**
  That's the girl **with** whom I went to the party. (very formal)
  That's the girl (who/that) I went to the party **with**. (less formal, more usual)
- **Who, whom, which, that can be omitted when there is a noun or a pronoun (*I, you, etc.*) between the relative pronoun and the verb, that is, when they are the objects of the relative clause.**
  Where is the ring (which/that) **George** gave you? (**Which/that** can be omitted.)
  The clock (which/that) **I** bought yesterday does not work. (**Which/that** can be omitted.)
  A person **who** repairs cars is a mechanic. (**Who** can't be omitted.)
  Note: **Who's = Who is or Who has** "Who's Charles?" "He's my brother"
  Whose = possessive I know a boy **whose** mother is singer.

Relative Adverbs (when, where, why)

Time	when (= in/on which)	2003 was the year **(when)** Peter was born.
Place	where (= in/on/at/to which)	That's the hotel **where** we stayed.
Reason	why (= for which)	Can you tell me the reason **(why)** he lied to me?

1 Fill in: *who, whose, which* or *where*.

My school, 1) ..... *which* ..... is called King Edward's, has about 2,000 students. My favourite
teacher, 2) .... is called Mr Brown, teaches sport. The sports centre,
3) .... I play basketball and tennis, is the largest in the area. I walk to school every
day with my friend Mike, 4) .... father teaches History.

2 Make sentences as in the example. Use relative pronouns or relative
adverbs.

- builder / someone / build houses
- painter / someone / paint pictures
- circus / place / can see acrobats

- tiger / animal / live in jungle
- supermarket / place / do shopping
- elephant / animal / ears are big

1 *A painter is*
someone who
paints pictures.

2 ....

3 ....

4 ....

5 ....

6 ....

15 Relatives

3 Fill in: who's or whose.

1 My mother, ... *whose* .... name is Elizabeth, is a piano teacher.
2 She's the woman . . . . married to an actor.
3 Céline is the girl . . . . brother won the prize.
4 Helen is the person . . . . car is outside our house.
5 Ann's the one . . . . a History teacher.
6 Lucas is the man . . . . helping us move house.
7 That's the woman . . . . son just graduated from university.
8 . . . . concert did you go to?

4 Fill in the correct relative pronoun. What part of sentence is each, subject or object? Write *S* for subject and *O* for object, then state if the relatives can be omitted or not in the box provided.

1 Did you see the man . *who / that* . stole her bag?
2 The dress . . . . Mary bought yesterday is too big.
3 Please give me the keys . . . . are on the table.
4 Is that the man . . . . we saw in the park yesterday?
5 What's the name of the lady . . . . babysits your little sister?
6 Klaus is playing with the dog . . . . lives next door.
7 Have you eaten all the cakes . . . . I made yesterday?
8 How old is the man . . . . owns that shop?
9 Have you met the man . . . . Jackie is going to marry?
10 Let's all look at the picture . . . . is on page 7.
11 Has Peter returned the money . . . . he borrowed from you?
12 What colour is the dress . . . . you're going to wear tonight?
13 The police arrested the man . . . . was driving dangerously.
14 The parcel . . . . is on the table is your birthday present.
15 We will ask the man . . . . delivers our milk to leave an extra bottle.
16 Is she the person . . . . gave you this CD?
17 We spent our holiday in a small town . . . . is near the sea.
18 The man . . . . married Kate is an actor.
19 Where are the shoes . . . . I bought this morning?
20 I still write to the old lady . . . . I met five years ago.

S	not omitted

5 **Write one word for each space.**

Hi Janet,

How are you? I'm doing all right. I just wanted to tell you 1) ....*about*.... something exciting 2) .... happened to me last Saturday. Do you remember Beth, 3) .... party we went to last winter? Well, I went 4) .... her and her cousin to a concert at Croke Park 5) .... my favourite band, Nickelback, were playing. Anyway, her cousin Rick knew someone 6) .... was working backstage and he let us meet the band. He even invited us to a party 7) .... the band was going to after the concert. It was amazing!

Now about the weekend hiking trip – the reason 8) .... I can't come is because my sister has asked me to take care of her children as she's 9) .... on a business trip. I'm so sorry. I was really 10) .... forward to it.

Write and tell me your news,
Shelly

6 **Complete the conversation using *who*, *which*, *whose* or *where*.**

Simon: Hi Nigel! Where did you go on holiday?

Nigel: I went to Greece. I had a great time there!

Simon: What did you do?

Nigel: I went to the Acropolis, 1) ....*which*.... is amazing. I also went to the place 2) .... the first Olympic Games were held.

Simon: Did you meet anyone interesting there?

Nigel: Yes, I met a girl from England, 3) .... grandfather was Greek. I also met her cousins 4) .... were staying in Athens. They made me feel very welcome.

Simon: It sounds like you enjoyed yourself!

Nigel: Yes, and I'm hoping to go back next summer.

Defining / Non-defining relative clauses

- A defining relative clause **gives necessary information and is essential to the meaning of the main sentence. The clause is not put in commas.** Who, which **and** that **can be omitted when they are the object of the relative clause.**
  People **who smoke** damage their health. The book **(which) my friend wrote** is very interesting.

- A non-defining relative clause **gives extra information and it is not essential to the meaning of the main sentence. In non-defining relative clauses the relative pronouns cannot be omitted.** That **cannot replace** who **or** which. **The clause is put in commas.**
  Mr Brown, **who lives next door**, went to Australia last week.

7   Fill in the appropriate relative, say whether the relative clauses are essential or not to the meaning of the main sentence, then add commas where necessary.

1 Paul Stevens, ... *who* .... starred in *Days,* went to school with my brother.   *not essential*

2 The pen .... I left on that table has disappeared.

3 The woman .... repairs our car is very friendly.

4 David .... grew up in Canada speaks French fluently.

5 The man .... car was stolen has gone to the police station.

6 Rye .... my grandmother lives is near the sea.

7 Oleg .... car has broken down is late for work.

8 The Coliseum .... attracts many tourists is in Rome.

8   Fill in the *relative pronoun* or *adverb*. Put commas where necessary. Write *D* for defining, *ND* for non-defining and if the relative can be omitted or not in the box provided.

1 Mr Brown, ... *who* ...... teaches us French, comes from London.	ND	not omitted
2 The girl .... I met on the bus looks just like my sister.		
3 Peter Smith .... had an accident is in hospital.		
4 The apples .... grow on these trees are delicious.		
5 This lemon pie .... I made yesterday tastes great.		
6 The film .... I saw on TV last night was very exciting.		
7 My friend Akim .... is a doctor works very long hours.		
8 John .... father is a lawyer has moved to Paris.		
9 The sports centre .... we play tennis is expensive.		
10 The vase .... Susan gave me got broken.		
11 The summer .... I went to Spain was really hot.		
12 The car .... tyres are flat is mine.		
13 The café .... I first met my husband has closed down now.		
14 Simon .... mother is a vegetarian doesn't eat meat.		
15 The bakery .... is by my house sells wonderful pies.		

9 **Match the phrases as in the example:**

1 a blender	a path at the side of the road	you relax in it
2 a party	something	you mix things with it
3 an armchair	a machine	people walk along it
4 a pavement	a piece of furniture	people enjoy going to
5 a fork	an event	you eat with it

1 *A blender is a machine (which) you mix things with.*
2 ....
3 ....
4 ....
5 ....

10 **Correct the mistakes.**

The town 1) ~~which~~ I was born has changed greatly over the last twenty years. Now, there is a modern shopping centre in the place 2) that my school used to be and all the children 3) whose went there have grown up and moved away. The local cinema, 4) that was built several years ago, used to be a dance hall 5) which big bands played. The park, 6) where was my favourite place as a child, is now a car park.

Some things are still the same though. Mrs Jones, 7) whom is now sixty years old, still works in the Post Office and Mr Jones still owns the baker's shop, 8) that his two sons now work. The hospital 9) where I was born in is still standing, although it is now much bigger than it was at the time 10) which I was born.

The day 11) which my family and I left our home town was one of the saddest days of my life.

1 ....*where*....	4	7	10 ....
2	5	8	11 ....
3	6	9	

11 **Complete the sentences so that they are true about you. Use *relative pronouns* or *adverbs*.**

1 The teacher *who / that I like most is Miss Jenkins.* ....
2 The singer ....
3 My favourite CD ....
4 The flat ....
5 .... was the year ....
6 The football team ....

15   Relatives

Explain the word

In teams, make sentences using *relative pronouns* / *adverbs*.

- watch / shows the time   • calendar / shows the date
- teacher / teaches students   • painter / paints pictures
- park / go for walks   • bus stop / wait for the bus
- CD player / plays music   • cinema / watch films

Team A S1:   A watch is something which shows the time, etc.

Speaking Activity

(Identifying things)

In pairs, take turns to say the name of a place, a thing or a person. Your partner has to explain what this place / thing is or who the person is.

A: theatre

B: A theatre is a place where we can watch a play, etc.

Writing Activity

Make sentences about yourself using *relative pronouns* / *adverbs*.

- (place) / meet my friends
- (place) / spend most of time
- (sport) / enjoy a lot
- (band) / like best

- (teacher / name) ... / kind
- (house / best friend) / live / near ...
- (sister / brother) / like ... / become ...
- (person) / love most

My school is the place where I meet my friends. ....

....

....

....

....

....

....

Reported Speech

 Listen and repeat. Then act out.

- **Direct speech is the exact words someone said. We use quotation marks in Direct speech.**
  He said, "I'll wait for you."

- **Reported speech is the exact meaning of what someone said but not the exact words. We do not use quotation marks in Reported speech.**
  He said that he would wait for me.

Say – Tell

- **We use say in Direct speech. We also use say in Reported speech when say is not followed by the person the words were spoken to. We use tell in Reported speech when tell is followed by the person the words were spoken to.**

Direct speech:	She **said to me**, "I am very tired."
Reported speech:	She **told me** that she was very tired.
Reported speech:	She **said that** she was very tired.

Expressions with say	say good morning, etc., say something, say one's prayers, say so
Expressions with tell	tell the truth, tell a lie, tell a secret, tell a story, tell the time, tell the difference, tell sb one's name, tell sb the way, tell one from another

---

1 **Fill in: *say* or *tell* in the correct form.**

1 The police officer ...... *said* ..... that the man was lying.

2 Philip .... it would probably rain tomorrow.

3 Susan ...., "Let's go out for dinner tonight."

4 Jim .... me about the party last night.

5 Our teacher .... he was pleased with our work.

6 Jane and Kate are twins. I really can't .... one from the other.

Reported Speech

Listen and repeat. Then act out.

We can report: A. statements   B. questions   C. commands, requests, suggestions

Reported Statements

- To report statements we use a reporting verb (say, tell, advise, explain, promise, etc.) followed by a that-clause. In spoken English that may be omitted.
- Pronouns and possessive adjectives change according to the meaning.
  Direct speech: He said, "I can't fix it **myself**."
  Reported speech: He said **he** couldn't fix it **himself**.
- Certain words change as follows :

Direct speech	this / these	here	come
Reported speech	that / those	there	go

Note that:
can changes to could
will changes to would
may changes to might
must changes to had to

"**This** is my book," he said. He said **that** was his book.

- When the reporting verb is in the past, the verb tenses change as follows:

Direct speech	Reported speech
Present Simple "I **want to** go to bed early," she said.	**Past Simple** She said she **wanted to** go to bed early.
Present Continuous "She**'s speaking** to Joe," he said.	**Past Continuous** He said she **was speaking** to Joe.
Present Perfect "I**'ve bought** you some flowers," she said.	**Past Perfect** She said she **had bought** me some flowers.
Past Simple "He **lost** all the money," she said.	**Past Perfect** She said he **had lost** all the money.
Future "I**'ll see** you later," he said.	**Conditional** He said he **would see** me later.

- **Time expressions change as follows:**

Direct speech	Reported speech
tonight, today, this week / month / year	that night, that day, that week / month / year
now	then, at that time, at once, immediately
now that	since
yesterday, last night / week / month / year	the day before, the previous night / week / month / year
tomorrow, next week / month / year	the day after, the next / following day, the next / following week / month / year
two days / months / years, etc., ago	two days / months / years, etc., before
"He arrived **last week**," she said.	She said (that) he had arrived **the previous week**.

- **There are no changes in verb tenses when the reporting verb is in the Present, Future or Present Perfect tense or when the sentence expresses something which is always true.**

Direct speech	She'll say, "I can do it."	"The Earth **is** round," said the teacher.
Reported speech	She'll say (that) she can do it.	The teacher said (that) the Earth **is** round.

- **The Past Continuous does not usually change.**

Direct speech	"I **was travelling** to Brighton while she **was flying** to the USA," he said.
Reported speech	He said he **was travelling** to Brighton while she **was flying** to the USA.

- **Certain modal verbs do not change in Reported speech. These are: would, could, might, should, ought to.**

Direct speech	"He might visit us," Mum said.
Reported speech	Mum said (that) he **might** visit us.

Reported Speech

2 Report what the guests said at a wedding last Saturday.

1 They'll make a lovely couple.

2 They're going to live in Brighton.

3 The bride and groom are very nice young people.

Mr Smith

Miss Moore

Mr Clarke

Mrs Jones

Miss Mayall

Mr Roberts

5 The couple's parents look happy.

4 The bride is wearing a beautiful wedding dress.

6 The bride's father has bought them a big flat.

1 Miss Moore *said (that) they would make a lovely couple.* ....

2 Mr Smith ....

3 Mrs Jones ....

4 Mr Roberts ....

5 Mr Clarke ....

6 Miss Mayall ....

3 Rewrite the following sentences in *reported speech*.

1 "New Year's Eve is always on December 31st," she said.
  She said (that) New Year's Eve is always on December 31st. ....

2 "The children are riding their bikes," Jennifer said to me.
  ....

3 "The Earth revolves around the Sun," the teacher said to the students.
  ....

4 "Jack and Karen have bought a house in the countryside," Nick said to us.
  ....

5 "Burglars broke into the museum last night," the news reporter said.
  ....

6 "Dad was mowing the lawn while I was cleaning the car," Ryan said.
  ....

7 "We will have a housewarming party next week," said Mike and Helen.
  ....

8 "Julia and José might move to Australia next year," Rory said to us.
  ....

Reported Questions

In Reported questions we use affirmative word order and the question mark is omitted. To report a wh-question, we use ask followed by the question word (who, what, etc.). When there is no question word in direct questions, if or whether is used in Reported questions. Pronouns, possessive adjectives, tenses, time expressions, etc. change as in statements.

Direct speech	He asked, "What time is it?"	He asked me, "Do you know her?"
Reported speech	He asked **what** time it was.	He asked me **if** / **whether** I knew her.

4 Turn the following into *reported questions* as in the example:

1 "What are you doing?" she asked her son.
She asked her son what he was doing.

2 "Do you like my new clothes?" she asked her friend.

.....

3 "Where are my keys?" he asked his wife.

.....

4 "Who is your favourite singer?" Mike asked me.

.....

5 "Where were you?" Barbara asked him.

.....

6 "Can you pick me up after school?" she asked her mother.

.....

7 "Have you seen Kim?" David asked Sarah.

.....

8 "When will you return?" Tom asked her.

.....

5 Report the police officer's questions to the shop owner.

1 What's your name?
2 Did you see the robbers?
3 What were they wearing?
4 How do you think they got in?
5 What did they take?
6 Has this ever happened before?

1 *The police officer asked him what his name was.*

2 .....

3 .....

4 .....

5 .....

6 .....

16 Reported Speech

Reported Commands / Requests / Suggestions

To report commands, requests, suggestions, etc. we use a reporting verb (order, ask, tell, beg, suggest,* etc.) followed by *to* infinitive or not *to* infinitive.

(*suggest is followed by the **-ing form**. e.g. He said, "Shall we go by bus?" He suggested **going** by bus.)

Direct speech	He said to me, "Get out of the house!" She said to me, "Do me a favour, please."	He said to me, "Don't touch it!" She said to him, "Please, please don't hurt me."
Reported speech	He ordered me **to get out** of the house. She asked me **to do** her a favour.	He told me **not to touch** it. She begged him **not to hurt** her.

---

6 Use the verbs in the list in the *past simple* to complete the sentences.

tell	suggest	beg	ask	order

1 "Close the door, please," Ann said to Jack.
Ann ....*asked*.... Jack to close the door.

2 "Let's go shopping," she said to me.
She .... going shopping.

3 "Please, please don't go," he said to Mary.
He .... Mary not to go.

4 "Get out of the car!" he said to them.
He .... them to get out of the car.

5 "Don't touch anything," she said to him.
She .... him not to touch anything.

---

7 Report what Mrs Lane told her daughter, Sue, to do.

1 Don't open the door to anyone!

2 Phone me if there's an emergency!

3 Don't let the twins eat any sweets!

4 Send the twins to bed at 9 o'clock!

5 Give the twins a bath before they go to bed!

6 Don't allow the dog into the twins' bedroom!

7 Close all the windows!

8 Put the toys away in the cupboard!

1 Mrs Lane told Sue not to open the door to anyone.

2 ....

3 ....

4 ....

5 ....

6 ....

7 ....

8 ....

8 **Turn the following sentences into *direct speech*.**

1 He said that he had ordered a pizza for dinner.

   "I've ordered a pizza for dinner." he said.

2 She said that they had to call their lawyer.

3 The plumber told them that he would go the following day to fix the tap.

4 She told her friend that was the best holiday she had ever had.

5 She asked him why he had said that to her.

6 She told them not to speak to their father like that.

7 He asked the secretary to show him where the manager's office was.

8 She told her son to take his books with him.

Reporting Verbs

Reporting verb	Direct speech	Reported speech
***to* infinitive** offer promise refuse	"Shall I carry the bags?" "I promise I'll be back early." "No, I won't buy you a computer."	He **offered to carry** the bags. He **promised to be** back early. She **refused to buy** me a computer.
+sb+*to* infinitive advise ask beg order warn	"You should see a doctor." "Could you feed the dog?" "Please, please help me!" "Go to your room." "Don't play with matches."	He **advised** me **to see** a doctor. She **asked** me **to feed** the dog. She **begged** me **to help** her. She **ordered** me **to go** to my room. She **warned** me **not to play** with matches.
+-*ing* form suggest	"Let's visit Sally."	"She **suggested visiting** Sally."
+that explain	"I'm going to stay with my sister."	She **explained that** she was going to stay with her sister.

9 Choose a reporting verb and turn the following into *reported speech*.

advised	asked	suggested	ordered	explained	promised	offered	refused

1 "I think you should exercise more," the doctor said to me.

The doctor advised me to exercise more.

2 "I will not answer your questions," the actor said to him.

....

3 "I really will phone this evening," he said.

....

4 "Let's go to the cinema," he said to her.

....

5 "Could you do something for me?" he said to her.

....

6 "Go to your room immediately and do your homework," she said to her son.

....

7 "You will be paid twice a month," her boss said.

....

8 "Would you like me to drive you into town?" she said to me.

....

10 Match the sentences in column A to the correct reporting verb in column B. Then rewrite the sentences in *reported speech* as in the example:

1	c	"No, I won't do it," she said.
2		"Let's go for a walk," he said.
3		"Please, please don't hurt me!" she said to the robber.
4		"Don't go near the campfire because it's dangerous," she said to Ben.
5		"I'll buy you a bicycle for your birthday," his father said.

a warn
b beg
c refuse
d promise
e suggest

1 *She refused to do it.* ....

2 ....

3 ....

4 ....

5 ....

11 First state if the following statements are true *(T)* or false *(F)* then turn them into *reported speech*.

1 "Penguins can swim," he said.

   He said (that) penguins can swim. .... | T

2 "The Earth is flat," the old man said.

   ....

3 "The cheetah is the fastest animal in the world," she said.

   ....

4 "A train goes faster than a plane," he said.

   ....

5 "Dolphins are less intelligent than sharks," he said.

   ....

6 "Man does not live forever," she said.

   ....

12 Write what the family said at the dinner table.

1 Does anyone want some more potatoes?

2 Pass me the orange juice, please Beth.

3 The chicken is very tasty.

4 I'm going to start my diet tomorrow.

5 Don't eat with your mouth open, Sam!

10 I don't want anything else to eat.

6 This is the best dinner I've ever had!

9 What are we having for dessert, Bob?

8 I'm very hungry because I only had a sandwich for lunch today.

7 Is there any more salad, Mum?

1 Mother *asked if anyone wanted some more potatoes.* ....

2 Father ....

3 Beth ....

4 Grandfather ....

5 Grandmother ....

6 Tim ....

7 Jean ....

8 Mark ....

9 Helen ....

10 Bob ....

16 Reported Speech

Whisper!

Students, in turn, whisper an untrue statement to the person sitting next to them. When a student can't report a statement or think of a new one he/she loses his/her turn.

S1: (whispers) I'm going on holiday next week.
S2: He said he was going on holiday the following week.
   (whispers) I have never eaten cheese, etc.

Speaking Activity

(Reporting people's words)

Work in groups. Imagine you are watching TV. Your partners are a reporter and a famous singer. Listen to their interview, then report it to the class. Use *reported speech*. Talk about:

- **how old / start singing**
- **when / make first album**
- **who / favourite singer**

- **how many songs / new album has**
- **which / favourite city**

- **how often / go there**
- **what / like doing in free time**

A: How old were you when you started singing?
B: I started singing at the age of twelve, etc.

The reporter asked the famous singer how old she had been when she had started singing. She said she had started singing at the age of twelve, etc.

Writing Activity

Imagine you are the reporter in the Speaking Activity. Write a short article for the magazine you work for using the information from the Speaking Activity.

This week's interview is with Mirella Rossi, the famous singer. I first asked her how old she

....
....
....
....
....
....

1 **Underline the correct item.**

1 That's the house **where** / **which** I grew up.

2 That's the woman **who's** / **whose** son won the Gold Medal.

3 This is the car **which** / **who** belongs to my father.

4 He is the actor **who** / **whom** won the Academy Award.

5 The girl **which** / **whom** you met at the party is my sister.

6 The reason **which** / **why** I didn't call you was because I came home late.

7 Tina will always remember the day **when** / **where** she graduated.

8 The house **which** / **where** was broken into is my uncle's.

9 The hotel **where** / **that** we stayed was near the beach.

10 I'll never forget the day **whom** / **when** I got married.

11 A butcher is someone **whose** / **who** sells meat.

12 The earrings **which** / **who** she gave me were very expensive.

13 That's the reason **why** / **which** she left early.

14 Jenny is the girl **who** / **which** won the competition.

2 **Fill in the appropriate relative, say whether the relative clauses are defining (*D*) or non-defining (*ND*), then add commas where necessary.**

1 Sally, ... *whose* ..... mother works at a bank, is my best friend. ..... ND .....

2 The book .... you lent me last week has disappeared. ....

3 Brian .... lives next door to me is going to Japan next week. ....

4 The shop .... I bought this dress is in King Street. ....

5 The woman .... house caught fire is in hospital. ....

6 The waiter .... took our order was very polite. ....

7 The Louvre .... is a famous museum is in Paris. ....

8 Carlo's Restaurant .... we have dinner on Sundays serves excellent food. ....

9 Mr Spencer .... you met last night owns an antique shop. ....

10 The day .... my son was born was the happiest day of my life. ....

11 The bank .... is near my house was robbed yesterday. ....

12 Jeremy .... lives next door comes from Scotland. ....

3 Fill in *say* or *tell* in the correct form.

1 The teacher ....*told*.............. us that we all passed the test.
2 John .... goodnight and left the room.
3 Grandma .... us a story every night.
4 Greg ...., "The match starts at 7:00 pm."
5 You should always .... your parents the truth.
6 Can you .... me how to get to the post office, please?

4 Write what the people said.

1 Joe ..*asked Sally if she could pass him the ketchup.*.............................
2 James ....
3 Chen ....
4 Peter ....
5 Ted ....
6 Sally ....
7 Ricardo ....
8 Paul ....

5 Complete the sentences using the words given in bold.

1 Don't touch that wire," he said to me.

WARNED He *warned me not to touch that wire.*

2 "Where is my book?" she said to him.

ASKED She ....

3 "You should stop eating junk food," my friend said to me.

ADVISED My friend ....

4 "Put your hands up," the police officer said to them.

ORDERED The police officer ....

5 "Shall I help you with your homework?" my brother said to me.

OFFERED My brother ....

 Listening

6 🎧 35 Listen and tick (✓) the correct box.

0 Who is Kim's cousin?

A ☐   B ✓   C ☐

3 What will they get Sam for his birthday?

A ☐   B ☐   C ☐

1 What is Dan doing this afternoon?

A ☐   B ☐   C ☐

4 Where's Jill's watch?

A ☐   B ☐   C ☐

2 How is Tim going to the train station?

A ☐   B ☐   C ☐

5 What time will the friends meet?

A ☐   B ☐   C ☐

17

Prepositions – Linking words

 Listen and repeat. Then act out.

Prepositions of Place

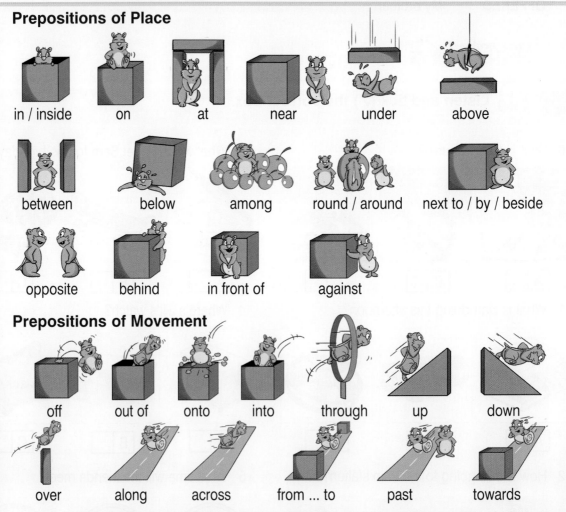

in + cities / towns / streets / the suburbs / an armchair / danger / the middle of / the queue

at + house number (at 23 Oxford Street) / home / school / university / work / the bus stop

on + the left / right / the floor / the outskirts / a chair / foot / holiday

by + bus / taxi / car / helicopter / plane / train / coach / ship / boat / air / sea

BUT on a / the bus / plane / train / coach / ship / boat – in a taxi / car / helicopter

1 **Look at the picture and fill in the gaps with a suitable preposition from the list.**

• behind	• next to (x2)	• on (x4)	• under

This is Judy's bedroom. She spends most of her time here. Her room is nice and large. There is a green carpet 1) .... *on* .... the floor. Her bed is very comfortable with a soft pillow 2) .... it. There is a window 3) .... the bed. 4) .... the bed there is a lamp. Judy's desk is very modern. There is a chair 5) .... it and some books 6) .... it. 7) .... the walls there are some pictures and a painting. There is also a small table 8) .... the painting.

2 **Underline the correct item.**

1 Tommy is the tallest **between** / <u>**among**</u> the students in his class.

2 We got **down** / **off** the train at Banbury Station.

3 Please walk **at** / **down** the stairs carefully.

4 Look, Aya is hiding **behind** / **under** the tree.

5 Jim is leaning **on** / **against** the wall.

6 The train is going **through** / **round** the tunnel.

7 When the bell rang, the children came **off** / **out of** their classroom.

8 Please leave your exam papers **on** / **in** the table.

9 Jennifer slipped as she walked **over** / **onto** the platform.

10 Is this the bus that goes from London **to** / **at** Oxford?

11 As I was walking **over** / **past** the bank, I saw Jill.

3 **Find the mistake and correct it.**

1 I live in 15 High Street. .... *at* ....

2 I go to school by foot every day. ....

3 Yesterday, Paul went to work on car. ....

4 Kim's office is at the fifth floor. ....

5 Kate is going to be late tonight. She's still in work. ....

6 They live at the outskirts of Madrid. ....

7 I met Alicia on university. ....

17 Prepositions – Linking words

4 Fill in: *in front of (x2)*, *between*, *behind*, *past*, *towards*, *in (x2)* or *against*.

There are lots of people 1) .....*in*.... the bank today. 2) .... the cashier's desk there's a long queue. Two cashiers are sitting 3) .... the desk. The manager is standing 4) .... the cashiers holding some papers. A guard is leaning 5) .... the cashier's desk. An old woman is walking 6) .... the guard 7) .... the cashier. A man wearing a hat is standing 8) .... the queue 9) .... a couple.

5 Fill in: *round*, *out of (x2)*, *on*, *above*, *into*.

Lisa and her friend, Dan, are having a great time at the Jelly Bee Circus. There is a lot to see. Beautiful horses are running 1) ....*round*.... the circus ring. An acrobat is carefully balancing 2) .... a rope 3) .... a juggler. He is throwing balls 4) .... the air. Dan is laughing at the funny clown who's chasing a monkey 5) .... the ring and Lisa is pointing at the circus magician who is pulling a long line of handkerchiefs 6) .... his pocket.

The circus is lots of fun!

Prepositions of Time

AT	IN	ON
at 8:15 am	**in** the morning / afternoon / night	**on** Sunday
at night / midnight / noon	**in** July (months)	**on** Monday evening
at the weekend	**in** summer (seasons)	**on** March 28th
at the moment	**in** 1991 (years)	**on** a winter's day
	in the twentieth century	
	in a week	

Note: **on time** = at the right time   **at 8:30 am** = exactly at that time
          in time = early enough, not late   **by 8:30 am** = not later than that time, before

6 Fill in: *at*, *in* or *on*.

1 ...*in*... the evening
2 .... Monday
3 .... midnight
4 .... April 13th
5 .... 5:30 pm

6 ..... Tuesday morning
7 ..... night
8 ..... 6:30 pm
9 ..... November
10 ..... the summer

11 1999
12 .... noon
13 .... the twenty-first century
14 .... Sunday morning
15 .... a spring day

7 Fill in: *at*, *on* or *in*.

1 A: What time is the seminar?
   B: It's ...*at*... 11:00 am ...*in*... the morning.

2 A: When do you finish your exams?
   B: .... two weeks.

3 A: When is your doctor's appointment?
   B: It's .... Tuesday morning .... 10 o'clock.

4 A: What days do you work?
   B: I work Monday to Friday from 9:00 am to 5:00 pm but I don't work .... weekends.

5 A: Is your birthday .... March?
   B: Yes, it's .... March 15th.

6 A: When did you last see Amanda?
   B: I saw her .... Friday.

8 Fill in the gaps with: *at*, *on* or *in*, then answer the questions.

1 What time do you get up ...*in*... the morning?
   I get up at 7 o'clock.

2 What time do you go to bed .... night?

3 What do you do .... weekends?

4 What sports do you play .... summer?

5 What do you do .... a cold winter's day?

6 Where were you .... 6 o'clock yesterday?

7 How old were you .... 2003?

8 What are you doing .... the moment?

9 Write one word for each space.

GRAHAM ZOO

| HOME | YOUR VISIT | ANIMALS | EDUCATION | EVENTS | MEMBERSHIP | SUPPORT THE ZOO |

Have Fun all Year Round 1) ...at... Graham Zoo!

Animals: The zoo 2) ...... over 5,000 animals, most are 3) ...... cages but some, visitors are able 4) .... touch.

Must see: Visit 5) .... Monkey playground. See the monkeys climbing, swinging and feeding high above the ground.

Zoo Opens: 6) .... 9:00 am daily.

Prices: Adults £9, children and students £6

How to find us: We are located 7) .... Grecian Park, near Riverdale Train Station. To get here 8) .... car take the M3 Motorway.

For more information: call us on (020)–774–6478.

10 Choose the correct answer.

1 Andy lives .... 75 Rose Street.
   A in   **B** on   **C** at ✓

2 Joan works in the building .... the bank.
   A below   **B** opposite   **C** under

3 Eric is travelling from London .... Cambridge tomorrow.
   A to   **B** into   **C** through

4 Don't worry, she'll be .... time.
   A at   **B** in   **C** on

5 Nathan had to go to the library .... foot.
   A by   **B** on   **C** at

6 José hung the painting .... the fireplace.
   A up   **B** under   **C** over

7 He promised to be back .... 4 o'clock.
   A in   **B** by   **C** on

8 They're building a new bridge .... the river.
   A along   **B** across   **C** onto

9 I arrived just .... time for my flight to Paris.
   A at   **B** in   **C** on

10 Ben is having a party .... Saturday evening.
   A on   **B** at   **C** in

Where is it?

A leader chooses an object in the classroom. In teams, students ask questions to find out where the object is.

Leader: (picture on the wall)
Team A S1: Is it on the teacher's desk?
Leader: No, it isn't, etc.

Speaking Activity

(Talking about location)

Look at the picture for three minutes. Then close your books and in pairs try to remember what there is and where it is in the room.

A: There is a table in the living room in front of the sofa.

B: The sofa is between two armchairs, etc.

Writing Activity

You've moved with your parents to a new house. Write a letter to your English pen friend describing your house both inside and outside.

Dear . . . . ,

I've just moved with my parents to our new house. It's very nice and I love it here.

My house is . . . .

Inside . . . .

My favourite room is . . . .

I expect you to come and visit me.

Love,

. . . .

17 Prepositions – Linking words

> Linking words **show the logical relationship between sentences or parts of a sentence.**

Positive Addition
and, both ... and, also
She's **both** clever **and** beautiful.

Contrast
but
Mary is talented **but** not very creative.

Cause / Reason
because, so
She took an umbrella **because** it was raining outside.

Condition
if, unless, or
He won't go to bed **unless** you tell him a story.

Purpose
to, so that
Sandra wrote down Helen's home address **so that** she could visit her the following week.

Time
when, as soon as, while, before, until, since, etc.
Diana called the police **as soon as** she realised that someone had broken into her flat.

Place
where
She couldn't remember **where** she had put her keys.

Relatives
who, whom, whose, which, what, that
That's the ring **which** once belonged to my great grandmother.

Listing Points / Events
- **to begin:** first, first of all
  First, I put on my pyjamas.

- **to continue:** secondly, then, next
  Then, I brushed my teeth.

- **to conclude:** finally
  Finally, I went to bed.

11 Join the two sentences using the word(s) in brackets.

1 I'd like to go to the party. I'm too busy. **(but)**
I'd like to go to the party but I'm too busy.

2 She jumped on a chair. She saw the mouse. **(when)**

3 She is studying hard. She will pass her exams. **(so that)**

4 It was cold. Tom put on a jumper. **(so)**

5 He's handsome. He's famous. **(both)**

6 Rick closed his eyes. He fell asleep. **(as soon as)**

7 Dan went to the hospital. He hurt his arm. **(because)**

8 I can't help her. I know someone who can. **(but)**

9 First, Jim washed his hands. Then he had lunch. **(before)**

12 **Read the sentences and underline the correct linking word / phrase as in the example:**

1 Maria put on the kettle **because** / **which** she wanted a cup of tea.

2 She won't speak to Bill **as soon as** / **unless** he apologises.

3 First, I prepared the meal. **Then** / **Finally**, I laid the table.

4 I haven't played handball **since** / **when** I left school.

5 **Which** / **Who** is the tallest person in your family?

6 Bob brushes his teeth **so** / **before** he goes to bed.

13 **Underline the correct linking word / phrase.**

Kelly is 9 years old. She has brown hair 1) **and** / **but** blue eyes. She is a very happy child 2) **who** / **which** likes to make new friends. All her teachers like her 3) **because** / **so that** she is very intelligent.

Kelly isn't only a great student. She's 4) **also** / **and** an amazing dancer. She can dance 5) **both** / **also** modern and jazz 6) **but** / **so** she especially likes hip hop.

14 **Choose the correct answer.**

Exercise is Great!

There are many good reasons 1) ..B.. we should exercise. 2) ...., it is great for our health. Playing sports, running, swimming and dancing help us build strong bones 3) .... muscles. Exercise 4) .... helps our heart get stronger.

5) ...., exercise makes us feel good about ourselves. We feel happier 6) .... we have more energy. We are able to run faster 7) .... become better at playing sports with our friends.

8) ...., exercise makes us look great, too. It helps us stay fit and keeps our body at a healthy weight, 9) .... is important for a long and healthy life.

	A		B		C	
1	A	what	B	why	C	which
2	A	Then	B	First of all	C	Finally
3	A	both	B	and	C	or
4	A	also	B	then	C	and
5	A	When	B	Since	C	Next
6	A	while	B	as soon as	C	when
7	A	or	B	and	C	both
8	A	Finally	B	First	C	Then
9	A	which	B	what	C	that

Articles

18

 Listen and repeat. Then act out.

> *Johnny, do you know where the Pyramids are?*

> *No, miss, they must be lost. There was a teacher here yesterday asking me the same question.*

| a + consonant sound (/b/, /d/, /g/, /f/, /l/, /p/, etc.) | a pen |
| an + vowel sound (/æ/, /e/, /ɪ/, /ɒ/, /ə/, etc.) | an apple |

- **A / An is used with singular countable nouns when we talk about things in general.**
  An aeroplane is faster than a train.   **A** greengrocer sells vegetables.
  (Which aeroplane? Aeroplanes in general.)   (Which greengrocer? Greengrocers in general.)

- **We often use a / an after the verbs 'to be' and 'have / have got'.**
  He **is** a photographer. He **has got** a camera.

- **We do not use a / an with uncountable or plural nouns. We can use some instead.**
  Would you like **some** tea? Yes, please! And I'd like **some** biscuits. (**NOT** Would you like a tea?)

- **A / An is not used before an adjective if it is not followed by a noun. However, if the adjective is followed by a noun, we use a if the adjective begins with a consonant noun and an if the adjective begins with a vowel sound.**
  It's a ring. It's **expensive**. It's **an expensive ring**.

- **The is used before singular and plural nouns, both countable and uncountable, when we talk about something specific or when the noun is mentioned for a second time.**
  The boy who has just left is my cousin. (Which boy? Not any boy. A specific boy, the boy who has just left.)
  There is a cat on the sofa. **The** cat is sleeping. ('The cat' is mentioned for a second time.)

- **We use the with the words cinema, theatre, radio, country(side), seaside, beach, world, weekend, etc.**
  We go to **the beach** every Sunday.

- **We use either a / an or the before a singular countable noun to represent a class of people, animals or things.**
  A / The dolphin is more intelligent than **a / the** shark. (We mean dolphins and sharks in general.)
  ALSO: Dolphins are more intelligent than sharks.

1 Fill in with *a*, *an* or *some*.

1 ....*an*.... apple

2 .... bananas

3 .... bird

4 .... cheese

5 .... diary

6 .... owl

7 .... egg

8 .... lemons

9 .... camel

2 Fill in: *a*, *an*, *the* or *some*.

1 A: Can I help you?
  B: Yes. I'm looking for ...*a*... book about whales.

2 A: When do you usually go to .... cinema?
  B: At .... weekend.

3 A: Do you have any plans for tonight, Mandy?
  B: Yes, I'm going out with .... friends.

4 A: Did you have fun at .... zoo?
  B: Yes! We saw .... penguins and .... elephant.

5 A: What do you want to be when you grow up?
  B: .... astronaut!

6 A: Where are .... boys, Bob?
  B: They are playing in .... garden.

7 A: Did you buy anything at .... shops, Betty?
  B: Yes, Mum. I bought .... silk scarf.

8 A: What's this?
  B: It's .... old radio.

18 **Articles**

The is also used before:

- **nouns which are unique.**
Haven't you been to **the Acropolis** yet?

- **names of cinemas** (the Odeon), **hotels** (the Hilton), **theatres** (the Rex), **museums** (the Prado), **newspapers** (the Times), **ships** (the Queen Mary).

- **names of rivers** (the Thames), **seas** (the Black Sea), **groups of islands / states** (the Bahamas, the USA), **mountain ranges** (the Alps), **deserts** (the Gobi Desert), **oceans** (the Pacific) **and names with ... of** (The Tower of London).

- **musical instruments.**
Can you play **the guitar**?

- **names of people / families / nationality words.**
the Smiths, the English, the Italians, etc.

- **titles without proper names.**
the Queen, the President

- **the superlative degree of adjectives / adverbs (the best).**
He's **the most intelligent** student of all.

The is omitted before:

- **proper nouns. Paula** comes from **Canada**.

- **names of sports, activities, colours, substances and meals.**
He plays **tennis** well. She likes **blue**. **Soda** isn't expensive. **Lunch** is ready.

- **names of countries** (Italy), **cities** (London), **streets** (Bond Street), **parks** (Hyde Park), **mountains** (Everest), **islands** (Cyprus), **lakes** (Lake Michigan), **continents** (Europe).

- **the possessive case or possessive adjectives.** This isn't **your** coat, it's **Kate's**.

- **the words 'home' and 'Father / Mother'** when we talk about our own **home / parents.**
Father isn't at **home**.

- **titles with proper names.**
Queen Elizabeth, President Kennedy

- **bed, school, church, hospital, prison,** when they are used for the reason they exist. John was taken to **hospital**. BUT: His mother went to **the hospital** to see him.

3 **Fill in *the* where necessary. Then circle the correct answer.**

QUIZ TIME

1 Is ..X.. Lisbon .the. capital of ..X.. Portugal?
(A) Yes   **B** No

2 Is ...... Malta in ...... Caspian Sea?
A Yes   **B** No

3 Is ...... Lake Baikal in ...... Russian Federation ...... world's deepest lake?
A Yes   **B** No

4 Where is ...... Sahara Desert?
A In Asia   **B** In Africa

5 What is ...... biggest island in ...... Greece?
A Corfu   **B** Crete

6 What is ...... capital of ...... Italy?
A Rome   **B** Milan

7 Is ...... Arctic Ocean bigger than ...... Indian Ocean?
A Yes   **B** No

8 Is ...... Everest ...... highest mountain in ...... world?
A Yes   **B** No

9 Where are ...... Sardinia and ..... Corsica?
A In the Black Sea
B In the Mediterranean Sea

10 Where is ...... Mississippi River?
A In the USA   **B** In the UK

172

④ Fill in *the* where necessary.

Did you know?

1 Rafflesia arnoldii is ..*the*.. largest flower in .... world. It weighs 7kg and grows only in .... Sumatra, Indonesia.
2 .... Johann Vaaler invented .... paperclip in 1899.
3 .... Badminton became an Olympic sport in 1992.
4 It took .... Egyptians 20 years to build .... Great Pyramids.
5 .... most important river entering .... Black Sea is .... Danube.
6 .... bass is .... largest of .... string instruments.

⑤ Fill in *a* or *the* where necessary.

John: Do you want to come to 1) ..*the*.. theatre with me tonight?

Ann: Sorry, I can't. I'm going to 2) .... restaurant with my cousin from 3) .... America.

John: What part of 4) .... USA does he come from?

Ann: He lives in 5) .... Colorado, near 6) .... Rocky Mountains. He's quite 7) .... famous musician. He plays 8) .... guitar in 9) .... rock band. In fact he's giving a concert at 10) .... Odeon in 11) .... Regent Street tomorrow evening.

⑥ Fill in *a*, *an* or *the* where necessary.

1 A: Can you tell me the way to ..*the*.. nearest bank, please?
   B: Sure. Turn left here and you'll find it in ...... Green Street.

2 A: Is this ...... Ahmed's motorbike?
   B: No, ... blue motorbike over there is his.

3 A: Where are ...... Wilsons going on holiday?
   B: They're going to ...... Bahamas.

4 A: What do you know about ...... Bermuda Islands?
   B: They're in ...... North Atlantic Ocean.

5 A: What shall we do tonight?
   B: Let's go to ...... Odeon. There's a comedy on with Jim Carrey.

6 A: I'm going to make .... pie for tonight.
   B: Great!

7 A: I saw ...... amazing film last night.
   B: Really? What was it about?

8 A: Brad is going to ...... London on ...... business trip.
   B: Is he going to stay at ...... Mandeville Hotel again?

9 A: Would you like some ice cream?
   B: No, thanks. I'd prefer ...... sandwich.

7 Lisa recently went on holiday to Spain. While she was there, she visited three different places, tried the local food and bought some souvenirs. Look at the pictures and the words given and say what Lisa did using *a*, *an*, *some* or *the*, where necessary.

go / Barcelona

......*Lisa went to Barcelona*......

eat / paella

....

buy / Spanish fan for herself

....

visit / Prado Museum

....

take photos of / Lake Sanabria

....

buy / flamenco dolls for her friends

....

8 Complete the questions with *a*, *an* or *the*, where necessary, using the words in the list. Ask your partner to answer the questions.

• **Mont Blanc**	• **breakfast**	• **UK**	• **African safari**
• ~~violin~~	• **restaurant**	• **aeroplane**	• **basketball**

1 A: Can you play ..*the violin*..?
   B: .*No, I can't but I can play the piano.*...........................

2 What do you usually have for ....?

3 Have you ever been to ....?

4 Would you like to climb ....?

5 Do you like ....?

6 Would you ever go on ....?

7 Are you going to eat at .... tonight?

8 Have you ever flown in ....?

Speaking Activity

Talking about a place

In pairs, ask and answer questions about where you and your family went on holiday last summer, which places you visited, what local dishes you tried and what souvenirs you bought for your friends.

A: Where did you go on holiday last summer?

B: We went to Venice in Italy, etc.

Writing Activity

You are writing a letter to your English pen friend. You are telling him what you and your family did on your summer holiday. Write about: what places / visit, what / eat and what / buy.

Dear ....,

I've just come back from .... We had a fabulous time there.

My family and I went to ...., which was fantastic. We ....

....

....

....

....

....

....

....

....

What about you? What did you do on your summer holiday?

Write back,

....

1 Fill in: *next to*, *beside*, *between*, *behind*, *against*, *across*, *in*, *over (x2)*, *along*, *on* or *under*.

Tai and his father are fishing

1) .....*beside*..... the river. Tai's dog is lying

2) .... him. His sister Lin is leaning

3) .... a tree. There is a boat

4) .... the bridge and a man

5) .... the boat. He is fishing, too.

There is a man riding his motorbike

6) .... the road. A man is driving

his car 7) .... the bridge. There is

a man 8) .... the motorbike. He is

walking 9) .... the road. There are some birds flying 10) .... the river and there is a girl lying 11) .... the grass 12) .... two trees.

2 Fill in: *at*, *on*, *under (x2)*, *in*, *behind*, *out of*, *opposite*, *in front of*.

1 The cat is .....*under*..... the table.

2 They are sitting .... each other.

3 Pedro is walking .... Juan.

4 Rosa is .... home. She is watching TV. She is sitting .... the armchair. The TV is .... her.

5 The woman is sitting .... the sunshade. The man is sitting .... the deckchair. The boys are coming .... the sea.

3 Fill in *at*, *in* or *on*.

1 ...*in*... the afternoon
2 .... August
3 .... Wednesday

4 .... noon
5 2005
6 .... September 12th

7 .... the weekend
8 .... spring

4 Fill in *the* where necessary.

1) ...—.... Cyprus is 2) .... third largest island in 3) .... Mediterranean Sea. It is located west of 4) .... Lebanon, south of 5) .... Turkey and north of 6) .... Egypt. 7) .... people who live there speak both 8) .... Greek and 9) .... Turkish. Cyprus is one of 10) .... most popular tourist destinations. Millions of tourists visit Cyprus every year.

5 Fill in *a*, *an* or *the* where necessary.

1 A: Do you know where ...*the*... Mississipi River is?
  B: Yes, It is in .... North America.

2 A: Have you ever been to .... New York?
  B: No, but I've been to .... Washington, D.C. and I met .... President when I was there.

3 A: Would you like to go to .... cinema tonight?
  B: I'd love to. There's .... great film on at .... Plaza.

4 A: We're planning to go to Spain this summer.
  B: I'm sure you'll enjoy yourselves. .... Spanish are wonderful people.

5 A: Which is faster, ... tiger or .... giraffe?
  B: I think .... tigers are faster than .... giraffes but cheetahs are .... fastest of all.

6 A: Did you know my cousin is .... actor?
  B: Really? I had no idea.

7 A: Is .... Mum busy at the moment?
  B: Yes, she is. She's making .... dinner.

8 A: Who is going to open the new hospital?
  B: I think .... Queen is going to do it.

6 **Underline the correct form.**

1 **Browns** / **The Browns** live in a beautiful house.
2 China is in **Asia** / **the Asia**.
3 Jimmy usually watches TV in **evenings** / **the evenings**.
4 Do you know how to play **guitar** / **the guitar**?
5 This is my best friend, **Pamela** / **the Pamela**.
6 **Sahara** / **The Sahara** Desert is in **Africa** / **the Africa**.

7 We have **dinner** / **the dinner** at 7 o'clock.
8 **Coliseum** / **The Coliseum** is in **Rome** / **the Rome**.
9 Let's play **volleyball** / **the volleyball**.
10 **The Earth** / **Earth** goes around **Sun** / **the Sun**.
11 We're going to **Canary Islands** / **the Canary Islands** for our summer holidays.
12 Austria is in **Europe** / **the Europe**.

7 **You will hear a man asking for information about buying a bus ticket. Listen and complete questions 1-5. You will hear the conversation twice.**

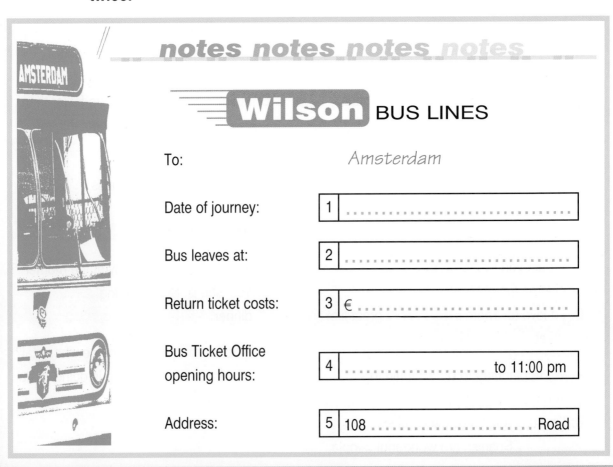

notes notes notes notes

Wilson BUS LINES

To:	*Amsterdam*
Date of journey:	1 ....
Bus leaves at:	2 ....
Return ticket costs:	3 € ....
Bus Ticket Office opening hours:	4 .... to 11:00 pm
Address:	5 108 .... Road

1 Put the verbs in brackets into the *present simple* or the *present continuous*.

Dear Akim,

I 1) .... (**write**) to tell you about the great time I 2) .... (**have**) with my grandpa in the countryside.

Every day, we 3) .... (**wake up**) early and we 4) .... (**start**) our day with a big healthy breakfast. Then we 5) .... (**go**) for a long walk by the lake. I really 6) .... (**enjoy**) it because there 7) .... (**be**) so many birds and animals here that you 8) .... (**not/see**) in the city.

Tomorrow, my grandpa and I 9) .... (**go**) fishing. He 10) .... (**have**) a small boat. I hope it doesn't rain.

See you when I get back,

Tom

(Points: ———)
(10x2   20)

2 Use the verbs to complete the sentences. Use the *present simple* or the *present continuous*.

see	belong	taste	have
not believe	cost	appear	think

1 This jacket .... a lot. It's very expensive.

2 She .... lunch now.

3 The food .... delicious.

4 I .... of going to the cinema tonight.

5 I .... George after work today.

6 This isn't Nick's laptop. It .... to John.

7 I .... what he's saying.

8 The band .... at the youth centre tonight.

(Points: ———)
(8x2   16)

3 Underline the correct item.

1 Beth **goes** / **is going** shopping every Saturday morning.

2 Mr Taylor **teaches** / **is teaching** Maths at Blair High School.

3 What **do you do** / **are you doing** tonight?

4 **Do Bob and Ann play** / **Are Bob and Ann playing** in the garden right now?

5 **Does water freeze** / **Is water freezing** at 0°C?

6 We **look** / **are looking** for some new furniture for our living room.

7 The Parkers **live** / **are living** in Manchester.

8 They **fly** / **are flying** to Rome tomorrow evening.

(Points: ———)
(8x1   8)

4 **Put the adverbs of frequency in brackets in the correct position in the sentences.**

1 I see my aunt and uncle because they live far away. **(rarely)** ....
....

2 Oliver is at school on time. **(never)** ....
....

3 Fiona watches TV in the evening. **(always)** ....

4 Sue spends her Saturdays with her friends. **(usually)** ....
....

5 Do you travel abroad? **(often)** ....
....

6 Jane plays in the park. **(sometimes)** .....
....

$\left(\begin{array}{c} \text{Points:} \ \dfrac{\quad}{6} \\ \text{6x1} \end{array} \right)$

5 **Fill in: has – have been in / to, has – have gone to.**

1 Belinda isn't here at the moment. She .....
....
the bank to take out some money.

2 Nigel and Layla ....
..... Mexico. They came back last week.

3 He ....
the garage for hours! What is he doing?

4 The Browns ....
Vienna on holiday. I'm sure they're having a good time.

5 Mrs Bowes .... Munich on business. She's coming back tomorrow.

6 Aya's sister ....
.... hospital since Wednesday.

$\left(\begin{array}{c} \text{Points:} \ \dfrac{\quad}{6} \\ \text{6x1} \end{array} \right)$

6 **Put the verbs in brackets into the present perfect or the past simple.**

Ann: I don't know where to go on holiday this year. Have you got any ideas?

Betty: 1) .... **(you/ever/go)** to Spain? I 2) .... **(go)** to Barcelona last year and I really 3) .... **(enjoy)** myself.

Ann: Well, I 4) .... **(spend)** two years in Spain while I 5) .... **(be)** at University. I 6) .... **(never/visit)** South America, though.

Betty: A friend of mine 7) .... **(work)** in Brazil before. I think you 8) .... **(already/meet)** her. Do you remember Kate from my party?

Ann: Oh, yes. I 9) .... **(speak)** to her. She's really nice. Maybe I can talk to her about it.

$\left(\begin{array}{c} \text{Points:} \ \dfrac{\quad}{9} \\ \text{9x1} \end{array} \right)$

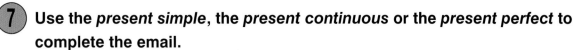

7 **Use the *present simple*, the *present continuous* or the *present perfect* to complete the email.**

Hello, Annie!

How are you? I'm so sorry I 1) .... **(not/write)** for so long but I 2) .... **(have)** a lot of exams lately. I 3) .... **(sit)** for three final exams so far this week and next week I 4) .... **(take)** a Maths and History test! Mr Jones, our Maths teacher 5) .... **(always/give)** us lots of homework – it 6) .... **(be)** very annoying but I know he only 7) .... **(want)** to help us! Anyway, how about you? When 8) .... **(you/sit)** your final exams? 9) .... **(you/study)** hard these days, too?

Well, I have to go now because Mum 10) .... **(just/call)** me for dinner. Please keep in touch!

Love,

Laura

Points: —— / 10x2 20

8 **Choose the correct item.**

1 Helen ..... a fax at the moment.

   A is sending   **B** sends   **C** has sent

2 They haven't seen each other ..... they left camp.

   A before   **B** for   **C** since

3 My mother ..... in a hospital. She's a nurse.

   A works   **B** is working

   C has worked

4 Have you called a taxi .....?

   A rarely   **B** yet   **C** just

5 He ..... in Italy before.

   A lives   **B** is living **C** has lived

6 He ..... his leg, so he can't play football.

   A has broken **B** breaks **C** is breaking

7 Paul ..... Paris for two years now.

   A has been to   **B** has gone to

   C has been in

8 Costas ..... a bath at the moment.

   A is having   **B** has   **C** has had

9 I haven't been to Portsmouth ..... three years.

   A since   **B** for   **C** just

10 They left the house an hour ....

   A last   **B** before   **C** ago

11 I've ..... tidied my bedroom.

   A already   **B** lately   **C** yet

12 He's ..... late for school. He can't wake up in the morning.

   A never   **B** always   **C** rarely

13 Yesterday, we ..... dinner at an excellent Chinese restaurant.

   A have had **B** are having **C** had

14 Janet ..... very pretty today.

   A is looking **B** looks   **C** look

15 Carla ..... two brothers and a sister.

   A has   **B** is having   **C** have

Points: —— / 15x1 15

Total: —— / 100

Revision 2 (Units 1–4)

1 **Put the verbs in brackets into the *present perfect* or the *past simple*.**

- A: How long 1) .... **(you/work)** for this company?

  B: I 2) .... **(start)** working here six years ago.
- A: Is this a new bicycle?

  B: Yes, my parents 3) .... **(give)** it to me last week.
- A: When 4) .... **(you/meet)** Alison?

  B: We 5) .... **(know)** each other since we

  6) .... **(be)** ten years old.
- A: Can you help me with the washing-up, please?

  B: I'm sorry, I can't. I 7) .... **(not/finish)** my homework yet.

$$\left(\begin{array}{c} \text{Points: } \underline{} \\ \text{7x3} \quad 21 \end{array}\right)$$

2 **Fill in: *have - has gone to, have - has been to / in*.**

- A: Can I talk to Mr Harris, please?

  B: I'm sorry but Mr Harris 1) ....

  .... Paris.
- A: Have you visited the National Museum?

  B: No, not yet. I 2) ....

  only .... Athens for two days.

- A: Are Sue and Ann at home?

  B: No, they aren't. They 3) ....

  .... the supermarket.
- A: 4) .... you ever

  .... New York?

  B: Yes and I had a great time.

$$\left(\begin{array}{c} \text{Points: } \underline{} \\ \text{4x1} \quad 4 \end{array}\right)$$

3 **Underline the correct item.**

1 Markus and Emma are listening to music **every day / at the moment**.

2 He **bought / has bought** a new computer last week.

3 I've lived here **since / for** 1987.

4 She usually **is visiting / visits** her grandparents on Sundays.

5 This time tomorrow, I **fly / will be flying** to Moscow.

6 Dad hasn't come home from work **already / yet**.

7 Don't go into the kitchen. I **am cleaning / have just cleaned** the floor.

8 Look! The Sun **is rising / rises**.

9 Lan **hasn't called / didn't call** us yet.

10 **Will you be going / Do you go** to the chemist's this afternoon? I need some vitamins.

11 This jacket **costs / is costing** a lot of money. I can't afford it.

12 Have you **ever / never** tried paella?

$$\left(\begin{array}{c} \text{Points: } \underline{} \\ \text{12x1} \quad 12 \end{array}\right)$$

4 **Rewrite the sentences in the correct order.**

1 plays / piano / she / the / beautifully ....
2 small / she / a(n) / antique / wooden / table / has ....
3 gave / me / he / beautiful / ring / a / gold ....
4 never / arrives / he / before / at work / 10 o'clock ....
5 goes / she / every / morning / jogging ....
6 by bus / to school / comes / usually / he ....

(Points: ——
6x2   12)

5 **Fill in: *than*, *of* or *in* and the correct *comparative* or *superlative* form.**

Martin Hamble is a member of one of the
1) .... **(famous)** basketball teams
.... the USA. He is 2) .... **(tall)**
and 3) .... **(young)** player ....
the team. Martin is a very good player but his friend, Jim, is
4) .... **(good)** .... he is.
Matthew Bodine is 5) .... **(old)** .... Jim
and Martin and he's also 6) .... **(fast)**
both of them. He is 7) .... **(exciting)** player to watch and also
8) .... **(popular)** member .... the team.

(Points: ——
8x2   16)

6 **Complete the exchanges with *too* or *enough* and the adjectives in brackets.**

1 A: Would you like to go for a walk?
  B: No, I'm .... **(tired)**.
2 A: Can he do the puzzle?
  B: Yes, he is ....
     (clever).
3 A: It's .... **(hot)** in here.
  B: Why don't you open the window?

4 A: Does your daughter stay at home alone?
  B: No, she's .... **(young)**.
5 A: Did they fly their kites on Saturday?
  B: Yes, it was .... **(windy)**.
6 A: Did you have fun at the party?
  B: No, it was ....
     (boring).

(Points: ——
6x2   12)

7 Fill in: *will/won't*, *shall* or *be going to*.

1 .... we go to the theatre this evening?

2 She .... probably pass her exams.

3 Now that he has the money, he .... buy a car.

4 Be careful! Otherwise you .... hurt yourself.

5 Look! Tim .... win! He's much faster than the other runners.

6 I'm afraid I .... be able to come to your party.

7 .... we go to Spain for our holiday this year?

8 She .... travel around the world. She's leaving on Friday.

9 I've just enrolled for the language course. I .... start it in September.

$\left(\begin{array}{c}\text{Points: } \underline{} \\ 9\text{x}1 \quad 9\end{array}\right)$

8 Choose the correct item.

1 He's ...... person I've ever met.
   A the friendlier   B friendly
   C the friendliest

2 The Moon ...... around the Earth.
   A is moving   B moves   C has moved

3 They haven't seen each other ...... they left school.
   A after   B for   C since

4 I think Holland ...... win the World Cup.
   A is going to   B will   C shall

5 My brother ...... to the gym. He'll be back in two hours.
   A goes   B is going
   C has gone

6 I haven't been to Portsmouth ...... three years.
   A since   B for   C after

7 You put too ...... sugar in my tea. I can't drink it now.
   A much   B many   C enough

8 Mike is ...... funnier than I am.
   A very   B less   C much

9 He ...... a new car last week.
   A bought   B buys   C is buying

10 This is ...... time I've spent away from home.
   A longer   B long
   C the longest

11 This time tomorrow, Kofi ...... for the airport.
   A leaves   B has left
   C will be leaving

12 My bag is ...... than hers.
   A the heavier   B heavier   C heaviest

13 I'm tired. I ...... to bed early.
   A go   B 'll go   C went

14 She ...... goes to the opera. She doesn't like it.
   A never   B always   C usually

$\left(\begin{array}{c}\text{Points: } \underline{} \\ 14\text{x}1 \quad 14\end{array}\right)$

$\left(\begin{array}{c}\text{Total: } \underline{} \\ 100\end{array}\right)$

1 **Put the verbs in brackets into the correct tense.**

Dear Bobby,

I 1) .... **(have)** great news! We 2) .... **(plan)** to visit your country! We 3) .... **(not/buy)** our plane tickets yet but we 4) .... **(think)** of coming at the end of the month. I'm so excited! We 5) .... **(want)** to visit all those places we've talked about.

Well, that's all for now. Talk to you soon!

Best wishes,

Mike

Points: ——
5x2   10

2 **Fill in the gaps with the correct form of the verbs in brackets. Use *be going to*, *was/were going to*, the *present simple* or *will*.**

Lea: What are your plans for the weekend?

Robert: We've just changed them. We 1) .... **(go)** camping but the weather forecast warned that it 2) .... **(rain)**, so we 3) .... **(stay)** indoors and watch some DVDs.

Terry: Do you have a few minutes, sir? I need to talk to you.

Mr Gear: I don't have time right now, Terry. I 4) .... **(be)** late for a meeting. I 5) .... **(see)** you when I 6) .... **(come)** back.

Terry: OK, sir. Thank you.

Paula: Are you busy this evening?

Wendy: Yes, I 7) .... **(watch)** a film with my friend, Sarah. Why do you ask?

Paula: I 8) .... **(ask)** you to have dinner.

Wendy: Oh. Well, I don't have anything planned for tomorrow.

Paula: OK! I 9) .... **(see)** you at 7 at Pierre's.

Points: ——
9x2   18

3 **Underline the correct item.**

1 Mitsuko is the best student **of** / **in** our class.

2 Their house is bigger **from** / **than** ours.

3 It's **much** / **more** hotter today than yesterday.

4 Ann is the shortest **in** / **of** Mary's friends.

5 The diamond ring is the **more** / **most** expensive of all.

6 Ivan is as tall **so** / **as** James.

7 The older she gets, the **more** / **most** beautiful she becomes.

8 The armchair is **much** / **more** comfortable than the chair.

9 This is **a** / **the** best film I've ever seen.

10 The Russian Federation is the largest country **of** / **in** the world.

Points: ——
10x1   10

Revision 3

4 Put the verbs in brackets into the *present perfect* or the *present perfect continuous*.

1 Don't walk in there! I .... (**just/clean**) the floor.
2 Jane's hungry. She .... (**not/eat**) since breakfast.
3 He is tired. He .... (**study**) for four hours.
4 I don't want to see that film again. I .... (**already/see**) it twice.
5 Sandy .... (**teach**) English for ten years.
6 Bruno .... (**not/do**) the washing-up yet.
7 He .... (**work**) all morning.
8 They .... (**play**) in the garden for two hours.

$$\left(\begin{array}{c} \text{Points:} \; \dfrac{}{16} \\ 8\text{x}2 \end{array} \right)$$

5 Put the verbs in brackets into the *past simple* or the *past continuous*.

My friend, Jill and I 1) .... (**walk**) home from school last week when we 2) .... (**see**) a little boy who 3) .... (**cry**). He 4) .... (**be**) lost and he 5) .... (**look**) for someone to help him. Jill and I 6) .... (**walk**) him back to our school and the headmaster 7) .... (**call**) his parents to pick him up. His mother and father 8) .... (**be**) very happy and 9) .... (**thank**) us for our help.

$$\left(\begin{array}{c} \text{Points:} \; \dfrac{}{18} \\ 9\text{x}2 \end{array} \right)$$

6 Fill in: *used to* or *didn't use to*.

When I was very little, I 1) .... spend a lot of time in my bedroom. I 2) .... play with my toys and watch cartoons. In the afternoons, I 3) .... go to the park with my mum. In the evenings, I 4) .... stay up late but now I do.

$$\left(\begin{array}{c} \text{Points:} \; \dfrac{}{8} \\ 4\text{x}2 \end{array} \right)$$

7 Underline the correct item.

1 His clothes are dirty. He **has been painting** / **was painting** the house.

2 The Millers **watched** / **were watching** TV when the lights went out.

3 This time next week, I **tour** / **will be touring** Rome with my family.

4 I **was going to call** / **called** you but I couldn't find your phone number.

5 Hilda **has been reading** / **has read** four books this month.

6 Dad **used to** / **didn't use to** work on Saturdays but he doesn't any more.

$$\left(\begin{array}{c} \text{Points:} \dfrac{}{6} \\ 6 \times 1 \end{array}\right)$$

8 Choose the correct item.

1 John .... down the road when he fell.
   A walked   B was walking
   C has walked

2 Jane is the .... person I know.
   A cleverest   B cleverer
   C more clever

3 She doesn't mind walking to work. She .... to it.
   A isn't used   B is used   C used

4 There are too .... books in this bag. It's very heavy.
   A much   B many   C enough

5 Janet .... the hairdresser's; she'll be back at 3 o'clock.
   A has gone to   B has been to
   C has been in

6 It's the .... coat she has ever seen.
   A most expensive   B more expensive
   C expensive

7 The weather is .... today than it was yesterday.
   A good   B better   C best

8 Don't worry. You will soon .... to wearing glasses.
   A are used   B get used   C used

9 .... breakfast every morning?
   A Do you have   B Are you having
   C Did you have

10 John .... rugby when he hurt his arm.
   A play   B played
   C was playing

11 I'll tell Luigi about the meeting. I .... him at work anyway.
   A have seen   B will be seeing
   C see

12 Tom sings ....
   A beautiful   B beautifully   C good

13 Frank is tired because he .... all day.
   A studied   B has studied
   C has been studying

14 Cathy .... move to LA but she decided to stay in Boston.
   A will   B is going to
   C was going to

$$\left(\begin{array}{c} \text{Points:} \dfrac{}{14} \\ 14 \times 1 \end{array}\right)$$

$$\left(\begin{array}{c} \text{Total:} \dfrac{}{100} \end{array}\right)$$

Revision 4 (Units 1-8)

1 **Put the words in the correct order to make sentences.**

1 She got up / suddenly / the room / and left

    ....

2 They've bought a / two-storey / lovely / in London / old-fashioned / house

    ....

3 He walked / in the rain / up the hill / slowly

    ....

4 Every Monday / to the gym / by car / they go

    ....

5 He's built a / wooden / beautiful / bookcase

    ....

2 **Choose the correct item.**

1 "Have you ever ...... Helsinki?" "Yes, once, in 1999."
   A gone to   **B** been to
   C been in

2 I ...... to driving on the left now but it was hard at the beginning.
   A 'm used   **B** 'm not used
   C used

3 While she was chopping onions, she accidentally ...... her finger.
   A cut   **B** has cut
   C was cutting

4 ...... your invitation to the wedding yet?
   A Don't you get   **B** Haven't you got
   C Didn't you get

5 He ...... live in London but now he lives in a small town.
   A uses   **B** used to
   C was used to

6 She ...... in this house for 25 years.
   A has been living   **B** lives **C** is living

7 Bruno and Carla are playing with two ...... children.
   A another   **B** the other   **C** other

8 They ...... have a barbecue but it started to rain.
   A will   **B** were going to
   C are going to

9 The black dress ...... Kim perfectly.
   A fits   **B** fitting   **C** is fitting

10 ...... you seen Nathan lately?
   A Have   **B** Did   **C** Do

11 They ...... house next week.
   A move   **B** are moving **C** moved

12 Ralph is ...... on time for work. He's never late.
   A often   **B** sometimes **C** always

13 Maria is ...... than her sister.
   A short   **B** shorter   **C** shortest

14 The soup is ...... hot to eat.
   A much   **B** enough   **C** too

3 Fill in the appropriate *reflexive* or *emphatic pronouns*.

1 Help .... to some more cake, please.

2 The children enjoyed .... at the party.

3 Nobody helped her with this exercise. She did it ....

4 Jack burnt .... while trying to make an omelette.

(Points: ——)
(4x2   8)

4 Fill in the correct *pronouns* or *possessive adjectives*.

My aunt and uncle live in Paris. 1) .... house is very big. They do most of the work 2) .... My aunt enjoys gardening and 3) .... friends say it is the prettiest garden in the world! At the moment, my uncle is painting the house 4) ...., and 5) .... friend, Mr Brown, is helping 6) ....

(Points: ——)
(6x2   12)

5 Fill in: *any, anything, no, nothing, some, somebody, somewhere* or *anywhere*.

1 Would you like .... chocolate?

2 I'm afraid there isn't .... juice left. Can you buy some?

3 Mei and I went shopping but we didn't buy ....

4 There is .... waiting for you outside.

5 Let's go! There's .... time to waste.

6 Are you going .... nice for your holidays?

7 I'm thirsty; I've had .... to drink all day.

8 I left my glasses .... in the house.

(Points: ——)
(8x1   8)

6 Fill in the gaps with *both, all, neither* or *none*.

1 A: Was the test difficult?
   B: Not really. I'm sure we .... passed.

2 A: How are Lin and Kim doing at school?
   B: Great. .... of them are very good students.

3 A: Are Tina and Kate at home?
   B: Yes. They are .... doing their homework.

4 A: Why didn't you and Maggie come to the cinema last night?
   B: .... of us felt like going out.

5 A: Why didn't you buy any of those trousers?
   B: Because .... of them fit me.

6 A: What do your parents do?
   B: They are .... teachers.

7 A: Mum, where did you put my books?
   B: They're .... on the table over there.

8 A: I'm looking for Camila and Sarah but .... of them is here.
   B: Yes. They've gone shopping.

(Points: ——)
(8x2   16)

Revision 4

7 **Put the verbs in brackets into the *past simple*, the *past continuous* or the *past perfect*.**

1 What ....
.... **(you/do)** at 8 o'clock last night?

2 They ....
(move) into their new flat two weeks ago.

3 We ....
(finish) tidying the flat by the time our guests arrived.

4 Tim .... **(turn)** 14 last Sunday.

5 The children were doing their homework while their mother ....
.... **(prepare)** dinner.

6 He couldn't pay the bill because he
....
(leave) his wallet at home.

7 When Dad ....
(come) home, we had dinner.

$\left(\begin{array}{c} \text{Points:} \dfrac{\quad}{14} \\ 7\text{x}2 \end{array}\right)$

8 **Put the verbs in brackets into the correct tense.**

1 After Mike ....
(pack) his suitcase, he called for a taxi.

2 Oh no! I ....
.... **(lose)**
my wallet!

3 The children are exhausted.
They ....
...... **(play)** all morning.

4 Helen ....
(cook) dinner before Tony came back from work.

5 Mitsuko's eyes hurt. She
....
.... **(read)** for hours.

6 He was happy because he
....
.... **(win)** the race.

$\left(\begin{array}{c} \text{Points:} \dfrac{\quad}{18} \\ 6\text{x}3 \end{array}\right)$

$\left(\begin{array}{c} \text{Total:} \dfrac{\quad}{100} \end{array}\right)$

1 **Rewrite the sentences in the correct order.**

1 always / writes / neatly / she   ....
2 owns / she / lovely / a / house / old   ....
3 I / TV / every evening / watch   ....
4 by bus / to school / goes / usually / she   ....

Points: ——
4x2   8

2 **Put the adjectives in brackets into the *comparative* or *superlative* form, adding any necessary words.**

1 Are there any .... **(many)** questions?
2 My brother is .... **(old)** me.
3 Is this dress .... **(expensive)** that one?
4 Tina is .... **(tall)** girl in her class.
5 That rock concert was .... **(good)** I've ever been to.
6 Trains are .... **(fast)** cars.
7 What is .... **(high)** mountain in Europe?
8 The Coliseum is one of .... **(famous)** monuments .... the world.

Points: ——
8x1   8

3 **Answer the questions using *too* or *enough*.**

1 "Can he have a shower?"
   "No, ...
   ...." **(cold)**

2 "Can he jump?"
   "No, ...
   ...." **(frightened)**

3 "Can he go to school?
   "No, ...
   ...." **(well)**

4 "Can he make people laugh?"
   "Yes, ...
   ...." **(funny)**

5 "Can he lift it?"
   "No, ...
   ...." **(strong)**

6 "Can Bob win?"
   "No, ...
   ...." **(slow)**

Points: ——
6x2   12

Revision 5

4 **Put the verbs in brackets into the correct tense.**

Dear Brenda,

How are you? I 1) .... **(write)** to tell you my exciting news! You 2) .... **(know)** how much I 3) .... **(always/want)** to be an actor. Well, my dream 4) .... **(finally/come)** true! Last week, I 5) .... **(try out)** for a small part in a film. And guess what! I 6) .... **(get)** the part.

To tell you the truth, I 7) .... **(be)** a little nervous about the whole thing but I do have a great acting coach. Filming 8) .... **(start)** in the next few weeks.

Wish me luck,

Ted

$$\left(\begin{array}{c} \text{Points:} \dfrac{\quad}{} \\ 8x2 \quad 16 \end{array}\right)$$

5 **Fill in: *both (of), neither (of), none (of)* or *all (of)*.**

Deborah and Carla are friends. They 1) .... like skiing and mountain-climbing but 2) .... them likes water sports, so they often go on winter holidays together. Last winter, they went to Switzerland with 3) .... their friends who like skiing and they 4) .... had a wonderful time. Unfortunately, 5) .... their friends could stay for more than a week but 6) .... Deborah and Carla are planning to go again this year. 7) .... them would miss it for the world!

$$\left(\begin{array}{c} \text{Points:} \dfrac{\quad}{} \\ 7x1 \quad 7 \end{array}\right)$$

6 **Circle the correct item.**

1 You **should** / **can** put your litter in the bin.

2 You **can't** / **don't have to** eat your lunch now. You can eat it later.

3 He **must** / **can't** be rich.

4 **Will** / **Shall** I help you with your suitcase?

5 **May** / **Must** I use your phone, please?

6 You **must** / **can** obey the school rules.

$$\left(\begin{array}{c} \text{Points:} \dfrac{\quad}{} \\ 6x2 \quad 12 \end{array}\right)$$

7 **Complete the dialogue.**

A: Hi, Sam.

S: Hello, Ali. That's my new bike over there.

A: 1) . . . . ?

S: My bike's the red one.

A: 2) . . . . ?

S: I got it last week.

A: 3) . . . . ?

S: Yes, it goes very fast.

A: 4) . . . . ?

S: It's a gift from my parents.

A: 5) . . . . ?

S: Yes, I ride it to school every day.

A: 6) . . . . ?

S: Yes, of course you can ride it.

(Points: —— 6x2   12)

8 **Add question tags and short answers.**

1 I've met you before, ... ? Yes, ...

2 I'm in the same class as you, ... ? Yes, ...

3 Her father's my Chemistry teacher, ... ? Yes, ...

4 He works hard, ... ? No, ...

5 You know about the bank robbery, ... ? No, ...

6 You've read the newspaper, ... ? No, ...

7 He lives next door, ... ? Yes, ...

8 She didn't pass her grammar test last week, ... ? No, ...

(Points: —— 8x2   16)

9 **Choose the correct item.**

1 Can I use . . . . . . mobile phone, please?

A you   **B** your   **C** yours

2 . . . . . . Penny use to live in Ireland?

A Is   **B** Does   **C** Did

3 May I have . . . . . . cup of tea, please?

A other   **B** another   **C** the other

4 Pablo speaks English very . . . .

A well   **B** better   **C** best

5 Does . . . . . . know where Pierre is?

A anyone   **B** no one   **C** someone

6 I'm hungry. I . . . . . . a sandwich.

A 'm having   **B** have   **C** 'll have

7 Elena made the cake . . . .

A herself   **B** himself   **C** myself

8 We're going to the cinema. Do you want to join . . . . . . ?

A we   **B** us   **C** our

9 "I'm going to the bus station."

" . . . . . . am I. I'll give you a lift."

A Neither   **B** Nor   **C** So

(Points: —— 9x1   9)

(Total: —— 100)

1 **Answer the questions using *too* or *enough*.**

1 "Can he eat his lunch?"

"No, ...

....

...." **(hungry)**

2 "Can you buy this necklace?"

"No, ...

...." **(expensive)**

3 Can Tim win the race?

Yes, ...

....

...." **(fast)**

$$\left(\begin{array}{c} \text{Points:} \quad \text{———} \\ 3x2 \qquad 6 \end{array}\right)$$

2 **Put the verbs in brackets into the correct tense.**

Last week, Pedro 1) .... **(start)** a new job in a computer company. He 2) .... **(work)** there for five days now and he really enjoys the work. He 3) .... **(find)** the first day difficult as he 4) .... **(not/do)** this type of job before. At the moment, he 5) .... **(look for)** a house near his office. He 6) .... **(hope)** he 7) .... **(find)** one soon.

$$\left(\begin{array}{c} \text{Points:} \quad \text{———} \\ 7x2 \qquad 14 \end{array}\right)$$

3 **Choose the correct item.**

1 Have you seen ...... glasses? I can't find them anywhere.

A your   B my   C mine

2 The ...... bicycles are in the garden.

A girls   B girl   C girls'

3 Silvio is a very clever boy, ... ?

A isn't he   B doesn't he   C didn't he

4 ......, we heard a loud noise.

A Sudden   B Suddenly

C More suddenly

5 This time next week, I ...... on a sandy beach.

A am sunbathing   B sunbathe

C will be sunbathing

6 Ian has lived in Rome ...... 2005.

A when   B for   C since

7 This cake ...... delicious!

A taste   B tastes   C is tasting

8 Cathy ...... to school when it started to rain.

A is walking   B was walking

C walked

9 That isn't ...... football. It's Tim's.

A my   B mine   C me

10 Did you ...... to play in the park when you were little?

A used   B use   C uses

11 When I got home, there wasn't ...... there.

A someone   B no one   C anyone

12 Sue ...... with her aunt this week.

A is staying   B stays   C stayed

$$\left(\begin{array}{c} \text{Points:} \quad \text{———} \\ 12x1 \qquad 12 \end{array}\right)$$

4 **Circle the correct item.**

1 You **can** / **should** buy a new car.

2 **Shall** / **Will** we go to the cinema?

3 You **mustn't** / **don't have to** talk during an exam.

4 You **can't** / **needn't** take an umbrella with you. The weather's fine!

5 She **can't** / **must** be his grandmother; she looks very young.

6 **Shall** / **May** I sit here, please?

(Points: ——
6x3   18)

5 **Complete the dialogue.**

J: Hello Mike. 1) . . . . ?

M: I'm going shopping.

J: 2) . . . . ?

M: I'm going with my friend, Melek.

J: 3) . . . . ?

M: We're going to buy some CDs.

J: 4) . . . . ?

M: Yes, I like pop music very much.

J: 5) . . . . ?

M: Yes, I do have Britney Spears' latest CD.

J: 6) . . . . ?

M: I bought it two weeks ago, when it was number 1 in the charts.

(Points: ——
6x3   18)

6 **Fill in the question tags in the dialogue.**

Eric: Let's go for lunch, 1) ....?

Lucy: Sounds great. Where would you like to go?

Eric: You like Mediterranean food, 2) ....?

Lucy: Yeah, I love it.

Eric: Then why don't we go to the Italian restaurant nearby?

Lucy: Good idea. It's right around the corner, 3) ....?

Eric: Yes. Hey, you've got Jane's number, 4) ....?

Lucy: Of course, why?

Eric: Let's invite her.

Lucy: OK. I'll call her right now.

(Points: ——)
(4x2   8)

7 **Put the verbs in brackets into the correct *infinitive* or *-ing* form.**

Georgia wants 1) .... **(become)** a teacher. She is a very good student who likes to spend time 2) .... **(read)** interesting books. During summer, she prefers 3) .... **(work)** at a camp. She enjoys 4) .... **(plan)** fun activities for the children. She is looking forward to 5) .... **(get)** her diploma next year. She can't wait 6) .... **(start)** teaching.

(Points: ——)
(6x2   12)

8 **Turn from *active* into *passive*.**

1) A farmer dug up a very old statue last week. 2) Somebody had buried it hundreds of years ago. 3) The farmer took the statue to a museum. 4) Experts are repairing it. 5) The museum will put the statue on display. 6) The museum has given the farmer a reward.

....

....

....

....

....

....

(Points: ——)
(6x2   12)

(Total: ——)
(100)

1 **Fill in the gaps using the appropriate tense.**

Sally 1) .... (**live**) in California. She 2) .... (**live**) there for five years. She 3) .... (**move**) there when she was seven years old. It was hard for her to leave her old school but since then she 4) .... (**make**) plenty of new friends. One morning, while she 5) .... (**wait**) for the school bell to ring, she 6) .... (**see**) a new student. The girl 7) .... (**stand**) in a corner and she 8) .... (**listen**) to some music on her MP3 player. Sally 9) .... (**walk over**) to say hello and the two girls started talking. Since then they 10) .... (**become**) great friends.

(Points: ——
  10x2   20)

2 **Choose the correct item.**

1 Your garden is larger than ....

  A us   **B** our   **C** ours

2 He's tired. He ..... since 9 o'clock.

  A studies   **B** has been studying

  C has studied

3 I want to go ..... hot on holiday. I think I'll travel to Spain.

  A nowhere   **B** anywhere

  C somewhere

4 She's at the bus station. She ..... travel by bus.

  A is going to   **B** will   **C** shall

5 I often drive my ..... car.

  A fathers   **B** father's **C** fathers'

6 It's ..... cold to go out.

  A too   **B** enough **C** more

7 When my older sister passed her driving test, she was pleased with ....

  A her   **B** herself **C** hers

8 I wish the neighbour's dog would stop .....!

  A barking   **B** to bark **C** bark

9 What ..... Pam doing yesterday at 3 o'clock?

  A was   **B** were   **C** are

10 May has four children but ..... of them are tall.

  A both   **B** neither **C** none

(Points: ——
  10x1   10)

3 **Put the verbs in brackets into the correct *infinitive* or the *-ing* form.**

1 I don't like .... by plane. (**travel**)

2 He left without .... goodbye. (**say**)

3 She managed .... a lot of weight. (**lose**)

4 .... helps you keep fit. (**swim**)

5 They asked him .... the truth. (**tell**)

6 Veena went to the library .... some books. (**borrow**)

(Points: ——
  6x2   12)

Revision 7

4 **Put the verbs in brackets into the correct tense.**

1 If she .... **(hurry),** she'll be on time for the meeting.

2 If he .... **(not/stay)** up late, he wouldn't have felt so tired.

3 If you .... **(go)** to the market, will you get me some fruit?

4 If you washed the car, it .... **(look)** much nicer.

5 They .... **(ring)** us if they had been in town.

6 If we work hard, we .... **(finish)** the project on time.

Points:
6x2   12

5 **Use the boy's thoughts to write conditionals.**

1 I don't have enough money. I can't take a taxi.

2 The weather is bad. I feel cold and wet.

3 I don't have a mobile. I can't call my parents.

4 I missed the bus. I left the party late.

5 The corner shop may be open. I'll ask to use their phone.

6 It's so dark. I feel scared.

1 ....
2 ....
3 ....
4 ....
5 ....
6 ....

Points:
6x3   18

6 **Complete the people's wishes.**

1 I wish I . . . .

He didn't see the toy car.
He tripped over it.

2 I wish I . . . .

She bought new shoes.
They hurt her feet.

3 I wish I . . . .

He wants to be good at football.

4 I wish I . . . .

It is very hot outside. Ted forgot his sun hat at home.

5 I wish my boss . . . .

Silvia's boss always gives her so much work.

6 I wish I . . . .

Charles doesn't want to see the dentist but he has to.

Points: —— 6x3   18

7 **Rewrite the following passage in the *passive*.**

1) Someone broke into the National Museum last night. 2) He broke the window. 3) He stole some valuable paintings and he destroyed a statue. 4) The police have found fingerprints on the walls. 5) They say they will catch the thief soon.

Points: —— 5x2   10

Total: —— 100

Revision 8 (Units 1–16)

1 Choose the correct item.

1 ...... I borrow you book?
   A Must   B Can   C Should

2 Mother's day is celebrated ...... May.
   A in   B on   C at

3 Tom ...... be at work. He isn't at home.
   A mustn't   B must   C can

4 Turn on the lights, ... ?
   A will you   B can you   C are you

5 I have two brothers. They are ...... tall.
   A all   B neither   C both

6 Would you mind ...... the dog out?
   A letting   B to let   C let

7 He comes from Russia, ... ?
   A does he   B isn't he   C doesn't he

8 The hotel ...... built in 1885.
   A is   B was   C will

9 This is my ...... new bicycle.
   A sisters   B sister's   C sisters'

10 They have been driving ...... four hours.
   A for   B since   C ago

11 Why are you always arguing with ...... ?
   A other   B each other   C another

12 I'll make ...... a sandwich.
   A mine   B my   C myself

13 Would you like ...... my holiday photos?
   A seeing   B to see   C see

14 I'll give it to her when she ...... back.
   A comes   B will come   C had come

$$\left(\begin{array}{c} \text{Points:} \, \dfrac{}{} \\ \text{14x1} \quad 14 \end{array}\right)$$

2 Underline the correct item.

1 Luisa **has to** / **doesn't have to** study hard if she wants to pass her final exams.

2 Jimmy **can't** / **couldn't** write when he was three years old.

3 **Will** / **Shall** I open the window?

4 She **can't** / **didn't need to** feed the dog as I had already done it.

5 **Can** / **Must** I borrow your pen, please?

6 You **shall** / **should** revise for your test.

7 Sean **was able to** / **could** climb to the top of the mountain.

8 You **ought to** / **might** have told him the truth.

$$\left(\begin{array}{c} \text{Points:} \, \dfrac{}{} \\ \text{8x1} \quad 8 \end{array}\right)$$

3 Turn from *active* into *passive*.

1) Somebody sent Jill flowers. 2) Someone left them outside her house. 3) One of her neighbours saw him. 4) He hadn't signed the card.

....

....

....

....

$$\left(\begin{array}{c} \text{Points:} \, \dfrac{}{} \\ \text{4x2} \quad 8 \end{array}\right)$$

4 **Use the boy's thoughts to write conditionals.**

1 I didn't save my pocket money.
   I couldn't buy Bob a present.

2 I lost the invitation.
   I missed his party.

3 I don't have his number.
   I can't call him.

4 Perhaps I'll see him tomorrow.
   I'll give him a birthday card.

1 ....

2 ....

3 ....

4 ....

Points: ——
4x4   16

5 **Complete the people's wishes.**

1 I wish I ....

Bob can't go out to play.
He has a temperature.

2 I wish I ....

David missed the bus
and now he has to walk.

3 I wish I ....

Sandra can't go to the party.
She has to work late.

4 I wish I ....

Mei's suitcase is very heavy.
She can't lift it.

5 I wish my son ....

Nikos can't work because his
son always plays his music too
loud.

6 I wish I ....

Liz lost her car keys and now
she can't drive her car.

Points: ——
6x3   18

Revision 8

6 Fill in: *why, where, who, whose, which* or *when*.

Dear Wendy,

   We're having a wonderful time here in Florida. Although the day was very hot
1) .... we arrived, now it's cooler. The hotel 2) .... we are staying is
lovely, and the staff 3) .... work here are very helpful. The beach, 4) ....
is right in front of our hotel, is beautiful and the water is so warm! I think that's the reason
5) .... so many people choose to stay at this hotel. We've also met a nice boy
6) .... parents own a yacht and tomorrow they're taking us sailing!
That's all our news. See you soon.
Love,
Alex and Layla

Points: ——
6x2   12

7   Write what the people said using Reported Speech.

1 Mrs Grady asked the shopkeeper ....
2 The shopkeeper told his assistant ....
3 The shop assistant said ....
4 Mrs Boyle asked the shop assistant ....
5 Mrs Kent told Tom ....
6 Tom asked his mother ....
7 Mrs Smith said ....
8 Mr Smith said ....

Points: ——
8x3   24

Total: ——
100

1 Choose the correct item.

1 I was hungry, ... I made a sandwich.

   A because   **B** so   **C** so that

2 That ring is gold. ...... one is silver.

   A Another   **B** Other   **C** The other

3 This jacket is the ...... in the shop.

   A more expensive   **B** most expensive

   C expensive

4 It rarely...... in the desert.

   A is raining   **B** rain   **C** rains

5 It's ...... warmer today than yesterday.

   A much   **B** very   **C** more

6 They have lived in Brussels ...... 2001.

   A for   **B** since   **C** ago

7 Dad ...... dinner right now.

   A makes   **B** make   **C** is making

8 I was hungry, so I made ...... a sandwich.

   A myself   **B** my   **C** me

9 She can't read ...... write.

   A and   **B** or   **C** but

10 She works in a bank, ... ?

   A does she   **B** isn't she

   C doesn't she

11 "I'm not going to work tomorrow."

   "...... am I. I've taken the day off."

   A So   **B** Neither   **C** None

$\left(\begin{array}{c}\text{Points:} \overline{}\\ \text{11x1} \quad 11\end{array}\right)$

2 Put the verbs in brackets into the correct tense.

1 A: Mum, where's Ramon?

   B: He .... **(study)** in his room right now.

2 A: Do you have anything planned for the weekend?

   B: Yes, this time tomorrow we .... **(sail)** in Lake Tahoe.

3 A: Why have you bought eggs?

   B: I .... **(make)** a cake.

4 A: Are the Millers still at home?

   B: Yes, they .... **(leave)** for Milan in an hour.

5 A: Have you seen Cécile?

   B: She .... **(go)** to the supermarket.

$\left(\begin{array}{c}\text{Points:} \overline{}\\ \text{5x2} \quad 10\end{array}\right)$

3 Put the verbs in brackets into the correct *infinitive* or *-ing* form.

• A: I want 1) .... **(buy)** Youssef a birthday present.

   B: Well, I know Youssef likes 2) .... **(listen)** to rock music. You could 3) .... **(buy)** him a CD.

• A: Can you come out to play?

   B: Sorry, I'm busy 4) .... **(clean)** my room.

• A: Do you have any plans for the summer?

   B: Well, David suggested 5) .... **(go)** to Greece for two weeks.

• A: What did your dad say?

   B: He agreed 6) .... **(let)** me go camping this weekend.

• A: I can't decide where 7) .... **(have)** my birthday party this year.

   B: Why not have it at Abigail's restaurant?

$\left(\begin{array}{c}\text{Points:} \overline{}\\ \text{7x1} \quad 7\end{array}\right)$

Revision 9

4 Turn from *active* into *passive*.

1) Someone started a fire in the National Park yesterday. 2) Luckily, someone called the fire brigade. 3) The police have arrested a man. 4) The police are still questioning him.

....

....

....

....

(Points: ——
4x3   12)

5 Underline the correct item.

1 Unless she **passes / doesn't pass** her exams, she won't get into university.

2 If I were you, I **would read / will read** the instructions first.

3 If Markus had gone to bed early, he **wouldn't have been / wouldn't be** late for school.

4 If I **want / wanted** to get fit, I would join a gym.

5 If you heat butter, it **melts / melted**.

6 If she had told me the truth, I **would have forgiven / would forgive** her.

(Points: ——
6x1   6)

6 Write what Brad wishes.

1 I want to go to Italy.

2 I don't earn enough money.

3 I want to be a footballer.

4 I don't have enough time to practise.

5 I shouldn't have joined a band.

6 I get home so late.

1 ....

2 ....

3 ....

4 ....

5 ....

6 ....

(Points: ——
6x2   12)

7 **Choose a reporting verb and turn the following into *reported speech*.**

offered	**promised**	**explained**	**warned**

1 "I won't tell anyone your secret," Tony said to Mei.

Tony ....

....

2 "I was late because I missed the bus," he said to his boss.

Rico ....

....

3 "Shall I help you with your homework?" he said to her.

He ....

....

4 "Don't touch the cooker," Dad said to me.

Dad ....

....

$$\left(\text{Points: } \frac{}{4\times3 \quad 12}\right)$$

8 **Fill in: *a*, *an* or *the* where necessary.**

Last summer we went to 1) .... New York. We stayed at 2) .... Ritz-Carlton Hotel. From our hotel room window we could see 3) .... Statue of Liberty. She is truly 4) .... amazing sight. While we were there, we visited 5) .... Empire State Building and 6) .... Museum of Modern Art. We also took 7) .... walk through 8) .... Central Park. New York is one of 9) .... most fascinating cities I've ever been to.

$$\left(\text{Points: } \frac{}{9\times1 \quad 9}\right)$$

9 **Fill in: *through*, *next to (x2)*, *in*, *on* or *under*.**

This is Sam's kitchen. He is standing 1) .... the cooker because he is cooking something. There are eggs 2) .... the frying pan. There is a clock 3) .... the wall. 4) .... the clock there is a shelf with some cookery books on it. Sam's cat is coming in 5) .... the window. Max, Sam's dog, is sitting 6) .... the chair, waiting for his breakfast.

$$\left(\text{Points: } \frac{}{6\times2 \quad 12}\right)$$

10 **Fill in: *at*, *in* or *on*.**

1 .... the weekend	4 .... night	7 .... a week
2 .... November	5 .... May 5th	8 .... noon
3 .... Sunday	6 2004	9 .... Friday evening

$$\left(\text{Points: } \frac{}{9\times1 \quad 9}\right)$$

$$\left(\text{Total: } \frac{}{100}\right)$$

205

Word List

A

ability
above
abroad
absence
Academy Award
accidentally
accordingly
accustomed
acrobat
across
act out
Active Voice
activity
add
addition
address
adjective
admit
adverb
advertisement
advice
advise
aerobics
affirmative
afford
African
against
agent
ago
agree
agreement
alarm clock
album
Algebra
alike
alive
allow
along
Alps
already
alright
although
always
amaze
amazing
ambulance
among
angrily
ankle
anniversary
announcement
annoy
annoyance
annoyed
answer the door
antique

any more
anyway
apologise
appear
apply for
appointment
appropriate
architect
area
argument
arrange
arrangement
arrest
Art
article
artist
aspirin
assistant
astronaut
at
at once
at present
at the moment
attach
attend
attention
attract
auxiliary verb
available
avoid
awful
axe

B

background
backstage
badminton
bake
ballet
bamboo
band
bank
bark
bass
be located
be used to
beach
beat
beauty
bee
beg
behave
believe
belong
below
beside
between
bike

bill
blender
blow
blow out
boil
bone
bored
boring
boss
both
bother
bowl
branch
break down
break into
bride
bridge
brilliant
broccoli
broom
brush
bully
bungee jumping
burglar
burglary
bury
bus stop
business
butcher
by

C

cabinet
calculator
calendar
cameraman
campfire
campus
cancel
capital
caramel
carefully
carelessly
carpet
cartoons
cashier
cashier's desk
cause
cave
ceiling
celebrate
celebrity
central heating
charge with
charity
chase
cheetah
Chemistry

cheque
chess
chest
choice
chop
circus ring
city
clause
client
clothing
cloud
clown
coach
coconut
colourful
column
comedian
comedy
comfortable
comics
command
committe
company
comparative
competition
complain
complete
completely
compose
concert
conclude
condition
conditionals
confess to
confirmation
confusing
congratulations
consonant
construction
contact lenses
contest
contrast
control
cool
cost
costume
cotton
countable
countryside
course
court
cousin
cover
crash into
credit card
cricket
criticism
cross

D

cuisine
curly
cycle

daily
damaged
dangerous
deckchair
decorate
decoration
deep
definitely
delicious
deliver
dentist
deny
derivative
desert
design
dessert
destination
diamond
difference
dig up
digital camera
dinosaur
direct
direct speech
director
disappear
discover
dishwasher
dislike
display
do the shopping
do up
documentary
down
driving licence
drop
drummer
dry
duration
during

E

eagle
earn
earring
easily
east
economical
effect
either
electric
elegant
email

emergency
emphasis
emphatic
empty
energy
enrol
enter
entertaining
environment
equivalent
escape
especially
essay
event
ever
everyone
everywhere
evidence
evil
examine
exciting
exercise
exhausted
exhibit
exhibition
expect
experiment
expert
explain
explanation
explore
explorer
expression

F

fabulous
fairy
fall over
falls
famous
fan
fancy
fancy dress
fascinating
favour
fax
feed
feel
ferry
fierce
fingerprints
fire alarm
fireworks
fit
fix
fixed
flamenco
flat

Word List

flat tyre
flavour
flight
float
floppy
fly
follow
following
for
foreign
forget
formal
formula
freeze
frequency
frightened
from ... to
fry
frying pan
funfair
furniture
further
further/farther

G

gallery
gardener
gardening
gate
general
gently
Geometry
gerund
get away
ghost
giant panda
give up
go off
government
graduate
grandson
greengrocer
greetings
groom
ground
grow up
guard
guide book
gym

H

habit
habitual
hairdresser
hall
hammer
hamster
handkerchief

handle
hard-working
hardly
hate
haunted
headache
headline
headmaster
healthy
heart
heat
heater
helmet
hiking trip
hip hop
hire
hockey
hoover
hope
hospital
housewarming
how long
how long ago
how many
how much
how often
however
huge
hurry
hut
hypothesis

I

ice-skating
imagine
immediately
improvement
in
in front of
in time
include
incomplete
indoors
infinitive
information
ingredient
inside
install
instead
instruction
instrument
intelligent
intention
international
interrupt
interview
into
intonation

invent
invite
iPod
ironing
irregular
irritation
issue
it's no use
it's worth

J

jam
jogging
join
juggler
jumper
junk food
just
just now

K

kettle
kindness
know
koala

L

laboratory
ladder
lamppost
language
laptop
last
lately
law
lawn
lawyer
lazily
leader
leading role
leak
lean
leather
leopard
let
lie
lift
light bulb
light fittings
lightning
limited
lined with
list
litter
local
lock
long hours
look for

look forward to
loud
lovely
loyal
luckily
luggage
lunchtime
luxurious

M

machine
magazine
manage
map
marshmallow
material
Mathematics
mayor
mean
medal
medicine
Mediterranean
melt
member
memories
message
mind
mobile phone
monthly
mop
motorbike
mountain range
move
mow
muscle
musician

N

name
national
naughty
near
nearby
nearest
neatly
necessity
negative
neighbour
neither
never
New Year
next
next to
nightclothes
noisy
none
nor
normally

north
note
now

O

obey
object
object to
obligation
obliged
obvious
occasion
ocean
off
offer
often
old-fashioned
Olympic
omit
on
on business
on foot
on the way
on time
on-the-spot
    decision
once
onto
opera
operation
opinion
opposite
orchestra
order
organise
out of
outer space
outskirts
over
oversleep
owl
own

P

Pacific
paella
painting
palace
palm tree
paper
paperclip
parcel
park ranger
part
part-time
partner
passive voice
passport

past
pasta
path
patient
pavement
pen friend
penicillin
pepper
perfectly
perform
permanent
permission
pet shop
petrol
    consumption
photocopy
phrase
physical
pianist
pick
pick up
picnic
pie
pillow
pilot
pink
place
plan
planet
plant
plastic
platform
playful
playground
pleasure
plenty
plumber
pocket money
pointy
polite
politician
pollution
polonium
pool
poor
popular
porter
positive
possession
possessive
possessive case
possibility
post
pour
prayers
prediction
prefer
preposition

Word List

present
present sb with
President
pretend
previous
price
prince
princess
principal
print
prize
probability
probably
produce
producer
programme
progress
prohibition
project
promise
promote
pronoun
proper noun
properly
pullover
pumpkin
punish
puppy
purpose
purse
put on
put up
puzzle

Q

question
queue
quiz
quotation marks

R

race
rare
radio transmitter
radium
rain cats and dogs
raincoat
raise
rarely
rather than
reach
realise
reason
receive
recent
recently
reception

recommend
rectangular
reflexive
refuse
regret
regularly
relative
relaxed
relaxing
relieved
remember
repair
repeated
report
reported speech
request
respect
result
revolve
reward
ribbon
ride
rise
risk
riverboat
roar
roaring
roast
rob
robber
rock
rocking chair
roller coaster
roof
rooster
round
row
rude
rugby
run away
run out of

S

sadly
safe
sailing
salary
salt
sand
sauce
save
say so
scared
scarf
scary
Science
Science Fair

scientist
Scottish
scuba diving
sculpture
seat
second-hand
section
seem
seldom
sell
separately
sequence
several times
shake
share
shark
sheep
shine
shiny
shopping centre
shout at
shower
shy
sick
sightseeing
sign
silk
silver
simultaneous
since
sink
situation
size
skateboard
skating
skeleton
skydiving
slightest
slip
slope
smell
snowstorm
so
so far
solar
sometimes
songwriting
soon
sort out
sound
south
souvenir
space
speed
spicy
sponge cake
sponsor

sports centre
square
stadium
statement
stative verbs
statue
steal
steam
sting
stone
strangely
struck
subject
substance
suburb
successful
suffer
suggest
suggestion
suit
suitcase
sunbathe
sunny
sunshade
superlative
suppose
surf the Net
surprise
sushi
swing
system

T

tacos
tag
take care of
takeaway
talented
talk
tap
taste
tasty
team
technician
tell one from
    another
temperature
temporary
tent
terrifying
text message
then
there's no point
    (in)
think
threat
through

tidy
timetable
toffee
tomorrow
tonight
tool
top
torch
tour
tourist
towards
towel
tower
traditional
traffic light
trainer
transfer
treasure
treat
tree house
trip over
trouble
trumpet
try
try out
tunnel
turkey
turn down
turn off
twice
twins
twist
two-storey
type

U

uncountable
under
understand
uniform
United Kingdom
unknown
unless
unpack
until
up
upset
usually

V

valuable
vegetable
vegetarian
view
voice
volunteer
vowel

W

wake up
wallet
wand
want
war
warn
watch out
water
weather
weatherman
weighlifting
weight
welcome
well
west
wet
whale
what
what time
wheel
when
where
which
whisper
who
whom
whose
why
wide
wife
wild
will
win
windsurfing
windy
wing
wire
wish
wonder
wooden
woollen
work out
world

Y

yacht
yesterday
yet
yoghurt